101 Ways to Earn Money

Dollars from Dandelions

Also by Helen Roney Sattler

Train Whistles: A Language in Code
Recipes for Art and Craft Materials
Jar and Bottle Craft
Jewelry from Junk
Sock Craft: Toys, Gifts, and Other Things to Make
Holiday Gifts, Favors, and Decorations
Kitchen Carton Crafts

101 Ways to Earn Money

Dollars from Dandelions

Helen Roney Sattler

Illustrated by Rita Flodén Leydon

Lothrop, Lee & Shepard Company
A DIVISION OF WILLIAM MORROW & CO., INC.

NEW YORK

Library of Congress Cataloging in Publication Data

Sattler, Helen Roney.
Dollars from dandelions.

SUMMARY: Suggests ways to earn money, such as service jobs, farm work, cleaning, pet and plant care and breeding, recycling, cooking and crafts, and running an exercise class.
  1. Vocational guidance—Juvenile literature   2. Youth—Employment—United States —Juvenile literature.   3. United States—Occupations—Juvenile literature.   [1. Occupations]   I. Leydon, Rita Flodén.   II. Title.
HF5381.2.S27   650′.12   79-11358
ISBN 0-688-41895-3
ISBN 0-688-51895-8 lib. bdg.

This book is
dedicated to
my sister,
Frances

Contents

Acknowledgment

I wish to express my thanks and deepest appreciation to all the people, young and old, who have so generously given me their time and shared their experiences to make this book possible.

Introduction

Do you ever wish you could earn some money? Then this book is for you. In it you will find more than a hundred ways young teen-agers have earned money. Some needed a regular income. Others wanted cash for special projects. This book tells how they found their money-making opportunities and suggests ways you can find your own. It helps to be in the right place when an opportunity comes along, but the real trick is to know an opportunity when you see it.

As the stories of these young people prove, anybody willing to work hard can find ways to earn money. Jobs are always available for good workers. Use your imagination and you will find them.

Earning money is something like climbing stairs. You start at the bottom and begin climbing. The younger you are when you take your first step, the better chance you have of reaching the top.

The first step is getting experience—most people prefer to hire experienced workers. You may be experienced without realizing it. Almost everyone has done unpaid work either at home or for someone else. Just as these young people used experience they got at home, so you can use yours. Choosing a job you like and can do well is good business sense because you will have more self-confidence and can perform better, which will help you get better jobs as you grow older.

101 Ways to Earn Money

Dollars from Dandelions

1

Outdoor Service Jobs

Providing services is a good way to earn money for special projects or extra pocket money. It is the best way to use experience you already have. Start by making a list of all the things you know how to do. What tasks do you do regularly at home? Have you done any volunteer work such as at a hospital or Society for the Prevention of Cruelty to Animals? Aided a sick neighbor? Now list places or persons that might need or be able to use similar services. You may discover money-making abilities you didn't know you had. At least you will have a place to start, and many possibilities. Look around your neighborhood. Find something that needs doing that you know how to do.

Use your creativity and imagination to think of new ways of utilizing your abilities and better ways of offering them to other people. As with sports, you need to out-think your competition to win. If you can't be better, you can be different or offer a better service—work harder and cheaper, giving your buyer more for his or her money. Everyone appreciates a bargain.

Asking for work

Everyone is scared when first asking for a job. Some are

better at hiding it than others. Practice not letting your fear show. The more experience you have, the less frightened you will be. Act self-confident even if you aren't. Be pleasant and cheerful, and always be neat and clean when asking for work.

Don't be discouraged if your services are turned down a few times. Not everyone is willing to pay someone to do something he can do himself. Not everyone can afford to. Keep trying. Sooner or later you will find someone who can't do it or would rather pay you to do the job than do it himself.

Where do you find employers?

Look for families without teen-agers or for people who can't or don't have time to do the many chores around their houses— the elderly, handicapped, ill or invalided; families where both husbands and wives work all day, families with preschoolers at home, or working single parents. Many of these people would hire someone to do certain tasks if they could find someone for a price they could afford. Those living on a fixed income usually cannot afford to pay the minimum wage.

These make good prospective employers of young teen-agers for such jobs as repairing or cleaning rain gutters, painting trim, putting up and taking down storm windows, mending fences, mending steps, patching sidewalks, or (if you live in an apartment house or walkup) washing windows and carrying trash cans to the curb. If you live at home, you have an advantage over adults seeking this kind of employment. You have free room and board and can afford to work for less. Make this advantage work for you while you are gaining experience.

How much should you be paid?

Only you can decide how much money you are willing to work for. But do discuss it with your parents or another trusted adult. They can keep you from being exploited or taken advantage of.

20

Have a clear idea of how much you think a given job is worth before you offer to do it. Find out how much others in your area are paid for a similar job. Be flexible. Keep in mind that many retired persons and low-income families can't afford to pay more than they have offered. You should be willing to work for a little less in order to get your first job. You can ask for more when you are experienced. Always find out how much you will be paid before you begin a job. Another thing to keep in mind: when you provide a service, you are paid to do a job. If it takes you twice as long to do the job as it takes someone else, you will be earning only half as much per hour as the other person.

Outside service jobs

Here is how eleven outdoor-lovers used initiative to create jobs for themselves where none existed. They saw something that needed doing and offered to do it at a reasonable price. Once hired, they worked hard and did a good job. This method worked for them. It will work for you.

DANDELION DIGGING—Twelve-year-old Richard's family couldn't afford to send him to Scout camp, so he set out to earn the money for the camp fee. Like many young people, he had no idea how to earn the $40 he needed. One day he heard his neighbor grumbling about the dandelions in his lawn and the backbreaking job of digging them out. Richard offered to dig up the dandelions for $3.

"The job is yours," said his neighbor.

Richard noticed that other neighbors had just as many dandelions in their yards. He made them the same offer and got their jobs. Then he looked for other yards with dandelions. For larger lawns or lawns with many dandelions, he asked for more money.

Not everyone he approached hired him, but he did his job well and before long he was receiving calls. His customers recommended him to their neighbors to protect their own yards from wind-blown seeds.

It was hard work, but Richard earned his $40 in six weeks. He made an extra $1.50 by selling three bucketfuls of dandelions to a man who wanted to make dandelion wine.

How to dig dandelions from a lawn

Although dandelions are cheerful spots of color loved by little children, they come close to being one of the most hated plants in nature. You, too, can turn them into money. Almost anyone with a lawn must deal with dandelions sooner or later. Some people resort to chemical sprays, but most people would rather pay you to dig them. Three dollars is much cheaper than sprays, and digging is more ecologically sound.

When you see a lawn full of dandelions, ring the doorbell and offer your services. Be businesslike and show you know what you are doing. You can use a special digging tool, but a long sharp knife will work just as well. Grasp the leaves of the dandelion with one hand. With the other push the knife or digging tool down at least four inches, close to the stem. Cut a complete circle around the stem, cutting the root as deeply as possible. Then lift the plant out. You must cut the root deeply or the plant will grow back. Practice on your own lawn or a vacant lot before you go looking for a job. Be careful when handling a sharp knife.

Another way you can make money from dandelions is by selling dandelion greens door to door. In many areas dandelion greens are a favorite food in the spring, not only because the tender young plants are delicious, but also because they are considered a spring tonic. You often can find large healthy plants, free for the picking, growing along roadsides or in

23

vacant lots. Collect only tender young plants—after the milk appears in the leaves they become bitter. Cut the plants off at ground level and tie (or use wire twisters) into bunches. You should be able to sell the bunches for 15¢ to 20¢ or maybe more in some areas.

SIDEWALK MANICURING—This chore is similar to dandelion digging. It is easy to see where the work is needed. Anytime you see a sidewalk overgrown by grass in the cracks or along the edges, you can be pretty sure the person living there either cannot do the job or dislikes doing it.

Unless the person is obviously living in poverty, ring the doorbell. Identify yourself and state that you are looking for work. Offer to trim the sidewalk for a reasonable price depending on the amount of work needed. As you gain experience, you will be better able to judge the time and effort required.

Don't be discouraged if you are turned down. Leave a card with your name and telephone number. Prospective customers

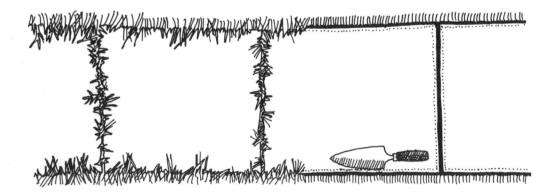

may say no today, but next week wish they had hired you. Sidewalk trimming is hard work, but there is little competition for the job.

Most employers will have the necessary tools for you to use. If your family has an edger you can use, that is the best tool for the job. A sharp spade or strong knife can also be used.

Take pride in your work. Trim the grass neatly along both edges of the sidewalk and get every blade of grass from the cracks.

If you live in an area without sidewalks, offer to trim along the curb, drive, flower beds, shrubs, or fencerows.

LAWN TENDING—Many kids find it difficult to ring doorbells and ask for work. If this bothers you, make up cards or flyers stating the kind of jobs you are seeking, your name, telephone number, and experience. Quote the price for each job you are willing to do. Make your cards appealing—let them express your personality. Remember that you are trying to sell your services. If the card is cute or funny, you make it easier for prospective customers to remember you. This is the way one boy did it:

LAWN TENDER
Your grass grows while you play.
I will cut, trim, and water it
While you are away
for $4 per week
Larry Moser   333-6542

He left a card at every house in his neighborhood and soon had enough work to keep him busy all summer.

OTHER YARDWORK—Lawn care has become big business in some areas and you can cash in on this. If you live in an apartment, you can probably walk or ride a bike to areas with lawns. Most customers have all the equipment you need.

Other types of yardwork for which you might apply are raking leaves in the fall and shoveling snow in winter. Many people take winter vacations and don't want snow accumulating on drives and sidewalks to advertise that the house is unoccupied. They need someone to shovel the snow while they are away. If you know people who usually go away for several weeks each winter, contract to do this job for them.

You can clean trash and leaves from flower beds in spring, and weed the beds in summer. This doesn't require experience, but you do need to know the difference between a flower and a weed!

You can trim hedges if you have had experience, or water lawns, gardens, and flower beds for vacationing neighbors. Lawn mowing can be done either on a regular basis or on a one-time basis for people on vacation. You will find more people who want their grass clipped while they are away than people who want it cut regularly. You can also take in mail and pick up daily newspapers for vacationers. For people who have their mail held at the post office and cancel the newspaper delivery, you can perform a service in keeping an eye on the house. Delivery notices stuck in doors, telephone books left lying on the doormat, and newspaper ads and flyers for local stores are a dead giveaway that no one's home.

GROUNDS KEEPING—Do you know someplace such as a shopping center, fast food store, or convenience store that has a large amount of trash accumulating around it? If you do, opportunity is knocking. There is a good possibility that you can get the job of cleaning it up.

Most managers want to keep their places of business neat and tidy, but trash accumulates faster than they have time to pick it up. Ask the manager how much money he would pay you to do this job. Better still, name your own price. Keep in mind that he cannot afford to pay very much.

Bob gets paid for cleaning the lot at a drive-in hamburger place once a week. He uses a leaf rake to rake the trash into piles, then puts the trash into plastic garbage bags which the manager provides. He then places the bags in the store's trash bin.

If you live in an apartment building, talk to the manager about hiring you to keep the halls, stairways, and grounds cleared of trash. Someone must do this. Why not you?

HELPFUL HENRY—When sixteen-year-old Hank couldn't find regular employment, he made up handbills which he left at every house in his subdivision.

WANTED
ODD JOBS
Need rain gutters repaired or cleaned?
Fence or steps need painting or mending?
CALL HELPFUL HENRY
Phone—556-4798
I ALSO TAKE DOWN AND PUT UP STORM WINDOWS,
mow grass, shovel snow, weed, and trim.
Whatever your chore, I'll do for a reasonable price.
No job too small or too difficult.

Hank's mother acts as his appointment secretary while he is at school or working, which is most of the time. His calls are recorded in a notebook and first calls are first served. Small jobs are done after school; big jobs are scheduled for Saturdays. He gets all the work he can handle because his work is satisfactory and his fees are reasonable.

How to be a helpful Henry

1. Learn your trade. Help around home until you are experienced in almost every household chore.

2. Advertise your services, but only those in which you are experienced.

3. Tell your client when to expect you, then be there. If weather prohibits working, then call to set a new date.

4. Whenever you report for a job, be professional. Find out exactly what your client wants done. Go to work immediately. Show that you are capable. When you do a good job, your client will call you again and will tell others about you.

5. Keep good records of your calls so that you can schedule your time adequately. Take down name, telephone number, address, and type of job.

6. Set your fees according to the task performed. Give an estimate before you begin, based on your experience with a similar job.

SWIMMING POOL CLEANING—People who have swimming pools in their backyards consider them a chore to clean and sometimes don't do it as regularly as they should. Many of these people gladly hire reliable teen-agers to do it for them, if the teen-agers do a good job and charge a reasonable fee. At least that is what Carl, 16, and William, 15, found out. Since they had had plenty of experience cleaning their own families' pools, they decided to join forces and use their know-how to earn money through the summer.

They passed out flyers to pool owners in their area. Four customers contracted for the boys' services once a week for the entire summer. This kept the boys as busy as they wanted to be and gave them a steady flow of cash.

How you can do it

If you have had experience cleaning pools, this could work for you. You can clean pools on a one-time basis or regularly. Most customers can furnish their own cleaning equipment which you can use until you get established. Then you can buy your own if you prefer.

If you haven't had any experience, team up with someone who has. Or, you can get experience by helping someone clean his own pool several times. You can also get experience by volunteering to help clean a community pool or a pool for a non-profit organization such as a YMCA or Scout camp. You might be paid a little for helping, or you might just get the privilege of swimming in the pool. Even if you don't gain anything except the experience, it is worth it.

How to find customers

If there are few home pools in your area, you can try motels. Motel operators are good businessmen. If you clean their pools for less than they would pay someone else, and if you do it well, you will have a steady job. Talk to the manager early, long before the swim season opens. If you wait too long, somebody else will nab the job.

RESURFACING DRIVEWAYS—Armed with push brooms and squeegees, 16-year-old Randy and his 14-year-old brother Dennis earned hundreds of dollars one summer making cracked and deteriorated asphalt driveways look like new. They got their first job when their dad put them to work resurfacing their own driveway with a water-base sealer.

The job turned out so well that their neighbors stopped by to admire the work, and one hired the boys to resurface his driveway. From then on the boys were kept busy. Since most of the driveways in their community had been put in about the same time as theirs, the boys figured there were other jobs to be had. They went door to door offering their services.

First the boys gave a free estimate based on the length and condition of the drive and the number of hours they thought it would take to do the work. An average driveway took about 10 hours and cost about $120. They worked it out so that they earned $5 to $6 per hour. But they only averaged $4 an hour when they first started.

These boys provided a needed service in their community and it paid them well. They each cleared $1000 in one summer.

How you can do it

1. Look for older neighborhoods with deteriorating asphalt driveways.

2. Word of mouth plus a visible example of your work make the best possible advertising. If you can get the job of resurfacing just one driveway in a neighborhood, you have a good chance of getting more.

3. If you are not known in the neighborhood, make up flyers or cards similar to this one to leave door to door.

YOUR DRIVEWAY NEEDS REJUVENATING
That is our business
R & D RESURFACERS
Free estimates
Phone 336-8654

HOUSE NUMBER PAINTING—Ringing doorbells and asking, "Would you like your house number painted on the curb for a dollar?" is the way Brenda, 12, and Claudia, 13, sell their service.

The girls cashed in pop bottles to get enough money to buy a set of 3-inch number stencils and two cans of fast-drying spray enamel. With these packed in their bike baskets they pedal around the neighborhood ringing doorbells. If one neighborhood isn't responsive, they try another. Since they travel by bike, they can cover a large area. They average about $10 each in a 4-hour working day.

How to paint numbers on a curb

First the girls paint a white rectangle on the curb. To speed up this step, they cut a 4-inch by 12-inch hole in a piece of cardboard to use as a background stencil. Brenda holds the stencil against the curb and Claudia sprays on the white paint, stenciling the rectangle onto the curb.

While the paint dries, the girls position the house number stencils inside a similar hole cut in a piece of corrugated cardboard. "We could use the same stencil, but it would get pretty messy because the paint is still wet," Claudia explains.

By using corrugated cardboard, they can slip the edges of the number stencils inside the two thicknesses and the numbers are held firmly in place.

As soon as the white paint is dry enough not to come off

when touched, Brenda holds the number stencil over the white rectangle. Then Claudia stencils the house number onto it with black spray paint. They can finish an entire number in 10 minutes.

Handy tips:

1. This job needs to be done on a warm day, 70 degrees at least.

2. For spray painting, follow the instructions on the can. Be careful. Use short spurts. Don't use too much paint or it will run, take longer to dry, and will cost more.

3. These girls used white backgrounds with black numbers, but you could use a dark green background with white numbers or a yellow background with black numbers.

4. Practice on a cardboard box first. Then paint your own house numbers on the curb in front of your house before you go to work for others. Don't worry if you make a mistake. Let the paint dry and start over.

5. This job can be messy, so be sure to wear old clothes and carry a swab cloth. Plastic bags worn on the hands of the stencil holder will save a lot of clean-up time. Paint thinner, brush cleaner, or fingernail polish remover can be used to remove paint from hands.

6. Advertise your services by passing out leaflets, especially in neighborhoods where people are not responsive. Point out that it is easier for firemen, police, delivery people, and friends to find houses that have numbers painted on the curb. If you can get two or three in a neighborhood, the rest often go along.

Add your name and telephone number and ask to be called if the resident wishes to buy your service.

2

Folding Money from Farm Work

If you like fresh air and sunshine, you might enjoy doing farm work. Fourteen- to sixteen-year-olds can legally work during the summer in any farm job not listed as being hazardous. If you are over 16, you can be hired to do any kind of farm work.

Farmers and ranchers are nearly always short-handed, especially at harvest time. Most jobs are seasonal, but some can last all summer. Farmers recruit help wherever they can find it, usually in nearby cities. Some send buses or cars to the city to bring workers to the fields; some provide lodging for short-term employees; others expect hands to provide their own transportation.

Most farm jobs aren't hard or dangerous. Experience isn't necessary, just muscle and a willingness to work. Your back may get tired because many jobs require stooping and bending, but the pay is usually good and you develop your muscles and get a great sun tan. If you do a good job, you will be invited back to help next season.

How can you get a farm job if you aren't a farm kid?
Some kids get their jobs because they know a farmer or know

someone who knows a farmer. But there are other ways. You can check with farmers in your area. Ride out and ask them whether they have any work you could do. Many farmers advertise for help, so watch the help-wanted ads. Some hire through the State Employment Office, so sign up there. You yourself can advertise in your local newspaper. Some local newspapers run free ads in early June for teen-agers seeking summer employment.

You can go places where farmers go—grocery stores, feed stores, farm equipment stores, or stockyards. Many farmers go to town on Saturday. That is a good day to get acquainted with a farmer. Help him load his purchases. This will show him you are an eager worker. Ask him if he knows anyone needing help on a farm.

Ask the manager of the feed store if you can post a farm job wanted sign in his store. It could say something like this:

Strong sixteen-year-old
WANTS FARM JOB
for the summer
No job too small to consider.
No experience, but willing to learn.
Phone—223-4657

One boy wore a farm-work wanted sign and stood outside a grocery store that he knew farmers patronized.

Be just as neat, clean, and well groomed when asking for farm work as you would for any other kind of employment. If you must furnish your own transportation to and from work, make sure you have this problem solved before accepting the job. Also have a clear understanding of what you will be paid before you go to work.

Here's how several young teen-agers earned folding money doing farm work.

MAKING HAY—Sixteen-year-olds, Roy and David, were in the right place at the right time. A farmer came to town looking for help. Since he needed someone right away, he went where young people hang out and announced that he wanted to hire two pairs of strong young arms to help him bring in his baled hay from the field. That is how Roy and David got their jobs.

It was a short job, lasting only three days, but the pay was good and the farmer promised to call the boys again in three weeks when he had more hay to bring in.

Many farmers need help making hay, because hay needs to be put in the barn before it gets rained on. This is difficult for one person to do alone. If you have a strong back, add this to your possible farm job applications.

The boys advise, "Wear long-sleeved shirts and leather gloves when loading baled hay. Baling wire can tear bare hands."

FENCEROW CLEANING—Many farmers will gladly hire anyone they can get to keep their fencerows free of underbrush. Most are too busy to do it themselves.

Don and Tom H. ride their bikes to farms outside their home town and clear the brush from the farmers' fences along the road. They are paid by the job.

This is a good job for outdoor people who like lots of vigorous exercise. Most farmers supply the axes and buck saws required for the work.

If you are a junior Paul Bunyan type and have a friend interested in helping do this kind of work, look along the road for fencerows that need cleaning. They are easy to spot, but

POISON IVY

DON'T TOUCH →

you won't find many unless you take the side roads. Most farmers along well-traveled roads keep their fencerows tidy. When you spot one that is badly overgrown, knock on the farmhouse door and explain that you are looking for work and noticed their fencerow could use a manicure. Ask how much he would pay you to clean it up. This is hard work so be sure you have a clear understanding of what you will be paid before you begin. *Always* finish a job you start, no matter how tired you get. A bargain is a bargain. After your first time, you will know how much this job is worth to you.

Caution—

Wear long sleeves, long pants, and leather gloves. Be sure you recognize poison ivy when you see it. If you don't, ask the farmer to point out any patches of it that may be growing along the fence.

WOODCUTTING—There is a good market for fireplace logs in cities of all sizes. If you live in a wooded area you might get a job cutting firewood. Many farmers hire town kids to cut trees, saw them into fireplace lengths, stack, and haul the logs. That's the kind of work Berry and Mike do each summer.

If you happen to know a farmer, you are in luck. Talk to him about hiring you to cut wood, even if he never cut fireplace logs before. Tell him the going price for logs in your town or city. That should convince him it could be profitable. You could offer to cut the wood on shares. That is, you will cut it for half the wood instead of cash. You will be responsible for hauling and selling your half.

If you don't know a farmer, you can contact the persons who usually deliver wood in your area (they usually advertise in the newspaper). Write down their phone numbers and keep them where you can find them. Most wood is cut in late summer and early fall for selling during the winter months. So look ahead. Watch for phone numbers in the winter for next summer's

employment. These sixteen-year-old boys call about a wood-cutting job early in the summer. Berry has been cutting logs for the same man for three years. He enjoys working in the woods. He says the exercise keeps him fit for sports.

Warning—

Do not use chain saws or other power tools without adult supervision. They can cause serious injury.

BERRY PICKING—Ramona spent three weeks on a farm last summer. Sound great? "It was," she says, "and the best part was that I came home with more money than I had when I went." Of course, she had to work for it.

Thirteen-year-old Ramona is a berry picker. She lives in an area where strawberries are grown. Her job only lasts two or three weeks, but she is a fast picker and earns a lot of money. Strawberry pickers are paid a set amount for each box they pick. Therefore the amount earned depends upon the speed of the picker.

Other berries are harvested this same way. If strawberries aren't grown in your area, perhaps blueberries, raspberries, or boysenberries are.

It isn't difficult to get berry-picking jobs. There seldom are too many pickers. Many berries rot on the vines because there are not enough pickers. Although commercial farms often hire itinerant picking crews, individually owned berry farms hire local help when they can get it.

To get a job, watch for the berry farm's ads or locate the berry farms nearest you, well in advance of the season. Stop by the farm and ask how to go about getting on the picking crew. Leave your name and telephone number. Ask to be called, or call back yourself when the season begins.

FRUIT HARVESTING—Carlos, 14, lives in an area full of apple orchards. He gets paid in apples for helping take care of the trees in a "pick-them-yourself" orchard. He sells the apples from his garage. Last season he earned $100.

Other young people are hired for cash to pick apples, peaches, cherries, plums, grapes, and other kinds of fruit in regular orchards or vineyards. They often are paid by the number of basketfuls picked. A good picker can earn a lot of dollars in a short time.

Fruit picking is not difficult or dangerous work. If you live in a fruit-growing area, check the telephone directory under orchards or vineyards. Call the owners well in advance of harvest time. Ask if they hire teen-agers to help pick fruit. If one does, ask how and when to apply for a job on the picking crew.

Most fruit growers hire anyone they can get. They often complain that they lose money because they do not have enough pickers to pick their fruit.

Another way to make money from fruit is by picking fruit in a "pick-them-yourself" orchard. You get the fruit at a substantial discount. Then you can sell the fruit at the current market price. You will need capital to buy the fruit you pick and transportation for it. An older friend who drives would make a good partner. You will get a good return on your investment if you can sell all of your fruit without any spoilage. Peaches, pears, plums, and cherries will need to be sold quickly to avoid spoilage, but apples can be stored in a cool place for several weeks. You can also find small orchards which will let you pick fruit on shares.

Use your imagination to think of good ways and places to sell your fruit. One girl sold her apples to a small grocery store. A boy sold polished apples at football games. Another sold them outside a big office building. A girl freezes cherries then makes them into pies later. Then she sells the pies.

NUT HARVESTING—Fourteen-year-old Ray sells fresh pecan meats. He gets his whole pecans by picking nuts for a farmer "on the halves." That is, he gets half of all the nuts he picks. On a good weekend he can pick 200 pounds.

Sometimes he sells nuts in the shell. Sometimes he sells cracked nuts. But he makes more money from the pecan meats. "They aren't hard to pick out," he says. "I do it while I watch television." He can pick out a pound or more of nutmeats in an hour.

He sells most of his nuts by placing an ad in the free community paper a few weeks before Christmas. Sometimes he sells nuts from his dad's car in a shopping center parking lot.

"If I have more than I can pick out, I sell some whole to a grocery store," he says. "Either way, it is all pure profit—I have nothing invested but my time." He stores nutmeats in throw-away glass jars and coffee cans.

Most farmers with large nut groves hire young people to pick nuts "on the halves" or for cash. Walnuts, pecans, and hickory nuts fall to the ground when ripe and must be picked quickly or the squirrels carry them all away. Black walnuts have a soft juicy hull which must be removed. Some growers have a machine to do this. Without a machine, the job can be messy.

There is always a market for nutmeats. If you keep your price competitive, you will have no difficulty selling all you have. Whole nuts can be sold at produce stores or supermarkets as well as to individuals.

Charlie picks hazelnuts, which grow wild along roadsides in his area. He hulls them and sells them in 5-pound bags to customers.

VEGETABLE PICKING—When you pass rows and rows of vegetables or a fresh vegetable stand on the edge of town, do you ever think of them as an employment opportunity? Twelve-year-old Kurt and his fourteen-year-old sister Andrea did. They often went to a truck farm with their mother to get fresh vegetables. One day the farmer commented that his vegetables were ripening so fast he couldn't keep up with them. This was too good an opportunity for Kurt and Andrea to pass up. They asked if he would hire them to pick the vegetables. He did, and now he phones them whenever a crop is ready to be harvested. They report for work the next morning at 7 A.M. and work until 11 A.M.

"My back gets tired," Kurt says, "but I like working outside in the fresh air and sunshine."

"I like the hours," says Andrea. "It's cooler early in the morning and I have all afternoon to myself. Sometimes we get to tend the vegetable stand. I like that best."

There are many truck farms (places that grow fresh vegetables) located on the outskirts of all large cities. If you live within biking or walking distance of one of them, go out and ask the farmer whether he needs help harvesting the vegetables.

47

Or go to the wholesale produce market and talk to the farmers who bring in fresh vegetables.

There are many kinds of jobs on a vegetable farm: preparing vegetables for market; washing root crops such as carrots, beets, and potatoes; helping to deliver vegetables to regular customers or selling door to door, and tending vegetable stands.

WEED PULLING—Fifteen-year-old Philip and twelve-year-old Matt are "roguers." That's what a weed puller is called. They pull weeds out of grain fields for a large commercial grain seed-growing organization. The company recruits fifty or more twelve- to fifteen-year-olds each spring to do this kind of work. They send a bus to the city to bring the roguers to the fields where they work from 5 A.M. to noon, five days a week.

"I get up at 4 A.M. to catch the bus at a shopping center parking lot," says Philip. "First we learn to tell the difference between a weed and whatever grain plant we are working with at that time. Sometimes it is milo, sometimes soybeans, and sometimes some other grain. If weeds aren't kept out of the fields, their seeds become mixed with the grain seeds and that ruins the seeds."

It is much cheaper to hand-pull weeds than to try to separate weed seeds from grain seeds.

The boys applied for their jobs at the company office, which is located on the farm. Your telephone directory or chamber of commerce can tell you whether you have a similar organization in your area.

OTHER TYPES OF FARM WORK—Sometimes vegetable farmers hire help for pest control. Hand-picking insects is more ecologically sound than using insecticides, and farmers can advertise their products as being pesticide-free.

A ten-year-old boy spent one day a week picking potato-bug larvae off potato plants one summer. "It's a good job for short people like me," he says. "We are closer to the plants and can see the bugs better. We don't have so far to stoop, either."

Other boys and girls have earned money pulling worms and suckers from tobacco plants on privately owned tobacco farms. Most large commercially owned operations have full-time hands who do this work.

A grasshopper plague provided an opportunity to earn money for several Oklahoma youngsters one summer. Farmers hired them to walk down their rows of soybeans swinging butterfly nets. With each swing the net filled with grasshoppers which they emptied into barrels.

One twelve-year-old boy, who was too young to be hired as a harvest hand, talked the farmer who hired his brother into hiring him to carry fresh water to the workers in the fields. The farmer even provided him with a horse to ride.

In each geographical area there are different opportunities for finding farm work. Just be alert and recognize the possibilities in your area.

3

Clean Up
with Cleaning Work

Some people don't like working outdoors or can't for some reason. For them, indoor cleaning offers many opportunities. There are always more people looking for help than there are people looking for this kind of work.

Practically everyone has had home experience in some kind of cleaning activity. All these factors—a large number of available jobs, little competition, and previous experience—almost guarantee you a way to earn money, if you use your imagination.

You can specialize in one kind of cleaning job, such as dishwashing, window washing, furniture polishing, bathroom scrubbing, garage, basement, or attic cleaning, emptying wastebaskets and taking out garbage, or whatever else you do best or have had the most experience with at home. Or you can do general house cleaning.

Offer your services to neighbors and friends. Many homemakers are looking for people to help them with their housework. As with outdoor services, the elderly, the handicapped, invalids, working women, and mothers of small children are also likely employers.

Here's how six young teen-agers cleaned up by using their imaginations to create moneymaking jobs for themselves.

MINI-MAID HOUSE CLEANING—Fourteen-year-old Julie needed money for school clothes. Since house cleaning was the thing she'd had the most experience with, she found a job cleaning for an elderly lady once a week. It took Julie 2½ hours to dust, vacuum, scrub the bathroom, change the sheets, and mop the kitchen of a three-room apartment. She was paid extra to clean the stove and defrost the refrigerator.

Another girl earned money tidying up and washing dishes every afternoon for a neighbor who had broken both her elbows.

Girls aren't the only ones who can earn money house cleaning. A sixteen-year-old boy cashed in on this wide-open job market by printing cards and posting them on grocery store and laundromat bulletin boards:

HOUSE CLEANER FOR HIRE—
BY THE JOB OR BY THE HOUR
Call 334-4395

"Lots of my customers were surprised that I was a boy, but none of them were ever dissatisfied with my work," he said. "I have been helping my mom since I was ten. Lots of women like the idea of having a strong back to help lift and carry things during spring cleaning."

How to find cleaning jobs

Julie found her job by answering an ad in the newspaper. Since household help is hard to find, many people are happy to hire experienced teen-agers. You can also advertise. Many communities have consumer bulletins in which ads can be placed free. Give only your telephone number and the type of job wanted.

Many laundromats and local grocery stores have bulletin boards. Hand-print your message on a yellow card, or with red ink, or any other way you can think of to make it attract attention. Or advertise by word of mouth. Let people know you are interested in doing this kind of work. Ask them to tell others. You can also go door to door and leave a card.

On the job

1. Have a specified arrival time. Then be on time.

2. If you will unavoidably be late, call your employer. Stay late to make up lost time.

3. Be businesslike. Either hire out to do a specific job and work until it is finished, or agree to work a specified number of hours and work diligently and carefully for the full time. No goofing off. Remember, this employer can be a good reference for future jobs, no matter what kind of work it is.

4. If you are sick and can't work, call your employer. Offer to do the work on a different day.

5. Be sure you or your parents know the person you will be working for, or make sure your employer has good recommendations. No young person should go inside a stranger's house alone. One solution is to get a friend to work with you as a team. You won't earn as much, but you will be safer. Two can finish faster than one, so you can handle twice as many jobs.

6. *Always* leave your parents written information about where you will be working that day: name, address, and phone number of employer.

DISHWASHING—Mary K. had an unique way to advertise

her specialty and it paid off well for her. Just before Valentine's Day she cut out red paper hearts which she glued to lace-paper doilies. On the hearts she printed this message:

GIVE YOUR WIFE A DISHWASHER FOR VALENTINE'S
Hire me to come in every weekday evening
to wash the dishes and clean the kitchen
Reasonable rates.
Mary K.   Phone 883-5083

She gave one of these to the husband of every working wife on her block.

LAUNDRY SERVICE—Many people, especially working women and college kids, hate going to the laundromat. What a perfect opportunity for anyone looking for a way to earn money!

Thirteen-year-old Janice does laundry for six people who live in her apartment building. It takes Janice about 1½ hours to pick up the laundry, wash, dry, fold, and return it. Her charges depend upon the number of washer loads, but her earnings average about six dollars a week. By doing laundry for two customers at a time she increases her earnings per hour.

Marcie irons shirts. She started by ironing for a lady who broke her arm. Now she has five customers who bring the clothes to her and pick them up. She has all the work she wants because she charges less than other laundry services, does a good job, and is reliable and prompt.

Janice found her customers by knocking on doors. You could do that, or you could post a sign offering your services in your local laundromat. If you live in a college town, post signs in each dormitory. This is one boy's sign:

HATE TO GO TO THE LAUNDROMAT?
How much will you pay me to do it for you?
I'll pick up, wash, dry, fold, and return your laundry
for a fee.
Call Leon   Phone No. 546-9068

Good advice for laundry people

   1. Be prompt. Have a regular time to pick up and a regular time to deliver.

2. Make sure the customer is home when you return the laundry.

3. Collect your pay before you leave the laundry.

4. Pick the least busy time at your laundromat to make your work go faster.

5. If you can get three customers from the same building, do all their laundry at the same time to increase your hourly pay. Be careful to keep each person's laundry separate.

6. Ask your customers to include laundry lists in their baskets. Then check your list before putting each piece into the washer and when you take them out of the dryer.

7. Wash dark-colored clothes and white clothes separately.

8. Charge extra for hand washables. Read labels on all pieces for laundry instructions.

9. If you furnish soap and bleach, which you might need to do for colleges kids, charge extra to cover the cost.

10. A small coaster wagon is a handy way to carry heavy baskets. A deep grocery cart will hold laundry bags nicely and it's lots easier to wheel them than carry them.

SILVER POLISHING—Twelve-year-old Phyllis earns extra money polishing the family silver. One day a neighbor noticed the lovely shine on their silver and offered Phyllis the same price to polish her silver. Seeing the possibility of making still more money, Phyllis offered her services to other neighbors. She now has five regular customers who call her whenever their silver needs polishing.

Polishing silver can take up a lot of a housewife's time. If you have had experience polishing silver and know of friends or neighbors who have silver serving pieces or flatware, offer your polishing services to them.

WINDOW WASHING—

I *DO* WASH WINDOWS
By appointment
For squeaky-clean windows, call
Aaron Fry   Phone 666-4450
Free Estimates

Fourteen-year-old Aaron leaves this robot-shaped card at the door of each apartment in his building and posts one on the bulletin board in the laundry room. Aaron specializes in washing inside windows only and has several customers who use his services regularly every second month. He also gets calls from others during spring and fall cleaning. He has all the work he can handle in his free time on weekends.

Aaron charges 50¢ per window which includes opening the window and cleaning the sills. He figures he can do six windows in an hour.

Outdoor window washer

This is the way another boy made dollars washing windows. Paul lives in a subdivision with one-story houses. He contracted with his neighbors to wash only the outside of the windows for 35¢ per window.

First he sponges off the windows with warm vinegar water, then rinses them with a hose, and dries them with a chamois. For hosing down screens and rehanging them, he is paid extra.

How to be a window washer

1. Spring and fall are good times to ask for window-washing jobs.

2. Neighbors and friends of your parents are good prospec-

tive customers. Shopkeepers are also good prospective customers.

3. Some homeowners may want you to wash both inside and outside of the windows. This is best done with a partner, one partner washing the inside while the other washes the outside. You will save a lot of steps checking for missed spots.

4. Inside, you need to be more careful about spills, so you should charge more. Seventy-five cents per window would be very reasonable for doing both inside and outside. You might get more than that in some areas. Pay depends upon the size of the windows. Large patio doors and picture windows should count as two windows.

5. For greasy film on windows, ½ cup ammonia in a bucket of water is a good cleaner. Vinegar and ammonia are cheap. One bottle of either will clean a lot of windows.

6. Any lint-free rag can be used for drying.

7. Use a sturdy stepladder to reach the top of the windows. Stick to ground-floor windows. Second-story windows are too risky.

PARTY CLEAN-UP—If you live in an area where there are lots of parties and few maids, you have an excellent opportunity for earning money. Many hostesses who can't afford to hire out-side help on a regular basis are delighted to hire responsible teen-agers to wash dishes and clean up the kitchen after or during their parties. Sometimes they may ask you to help serve.

A fee for this kind of work depends upon where you live. You should earn more for cleaning up than for baby-sitting. Ask the hostess what she will pay you before you accept the job.

You can find clients just as you do for baby-sitting jobs. Your teachers, your parents' friends, and your neighbors are good sources. If you do a good job, you will be recommended to others. Let it be known that you are available and willing to do this kind of work.

Like baby sitting, however, these jobs are most often at night and during holiday seasons. This is something to keep in mind.

4

Helping Hands
Earn Hard Cash

Lending helping hands and strong backs to people in need has put cash into many young people's pockets. You need only use your eyes to see people in need of help. Shut-ins, the elderly, mothers of young children—all need help occasionally. There are many things senior citizens can no longer do for themselves. Many of them are too proud to ask for help. They welcome having a reliable young person stop by once a week to do those little things that have become too difficult to do. Use your ingenuity to think of new, creative ways to offer them the help they need.

You can find senior citizens who might need your help through your church or synagogue, or a senior citizens' center.

Here's how seven young people earned money lending helping hands.

GROCERY TOTING—Elderly people, especially those without cars, appreciate dependable strong arms to help carry heavy grocery bags. Even those with cars can use help carrying the groceries into the kitchen.

Thirteen-year-old Roger does this for three elderly neighbors who pay him 50¢ a trip. Whenever they plan to shop for a week's food supply they call Roger. He accompanies them to the store and helps carry the heavy bags of groceries home.

Roger says, "I volunteered my services a couple of times, then I offered to make myself available on a regular basis for a small fee. I don't ask for much because most old people don't have a lot of money."

If you would like to do this kind of thing, volunteer your services a few times. This is good business practice, just as many manufacturers give free samples to advertise their products. It won't cost anything except a little time, and it returns big dividends in good will.

Give your customers a schedule of hours and days on which you will be available and ask them to call you in advance when they are going to need you. It is best if you can set up a regular schedule for each customer.

SHOPPER—If you are fifteen or sixteen and have had experience shopping for your mother, you could shop once or twice a week for working women or mothers of new babies. Ask your customers to supply you with a detailed list giving brand names and sizes of all items needed.

ERRAND RUNNING—Twelve-year-old Andy is an errand boy for residents of a senior citizens' complex. He does almost anything, from going for the Sunday paper to getting bread or milk from the grocery store. He has mailed letters and packages, gone for pizzas, picked up dry cleaning, and returned books to the library.

"My grandmother lives in the senior citizens' home," says

Andy. "She has arthritis and can't walk well, so I go over once or twice a week and run errands for her. Some of her friends started asking me to do little things for them, too, and usually gave me a quarter for doing it. Then I got the idea of being the official errand boy for the whole complex. They call me Handy Andy."

He is paid for each errand. Since he can usually combine trips and go for several customers at a time, he actually earns more per trip.

How you can do it

1. You don't have to live near a retirement village to do this kind of work. If you own a bike, you can run errands for anyone. However, your most likely customers will be shut-ins, people without cars, working mothers, mothers of small children, and old people.

2. If you have several elderly neighbors who do not drive, offer them your services. Visit them first and get to know them. Let them see that you are dependable and trustworthy. You can also advertise and ask satisfied customers to recommend you.

3. Specify which days of the week and what hours you will be available for running errands. Then be sure you are available at that time.

4. Set your fee according to the number of miles you must travel.

5. Do not go into the houses of strangers. If you must wait for a return message or package, wait outside.

AGED PARENT OR SPOUSE SITTING—Lots of kids baby-sit. Cindy sits with the elderly.

PARENT SITTING
Need a break?
Reliable 14-year-old Candy Striper
will stay with your bedridden loved ones
while you go out to take care of business or just have fun.
Good references available.
Cindy Grant   363-4935

Cindy saw that a lot of people in her neighborhood had a real problem. They had bedridden elderly parents or spouses living with them and had to stay in the house day and night. So she left a flyer at their doors to offer her services.

"My customers really appreciate my help. They say it is hard to find a responsible person willing to stay with their loved ones," says Cindy.

Cindy has worked as a Candy Striper in the geriatrics ward of the hospital and understands the care and love needed by the elderly. Most of the time she reads or talks to them. "They have some interesting stories to tell," she says, "and they like to talk about their past. But some of them can't communicate and then I just sit beside them and read to myself."

Cindy charges by the hour. Most customers use her at least once a week.

How to find people needing this service

Your church, synagogue, or community center will have lists of bedridden members. You could also check senior citizens' centers.

DIAPER SERVICE—If you live in or near an apartment building or complex or in a neighborhood where there are many babies or toddlers still in diapers, why not start a diaper service? That's what Judy did.

"New mothers are buried under piles of laundry. Lots of them don't have washers and it is difficult for them to go to the laundromat. That's why I don't have any trouble finding customers," she says. "Some use disposable diapers, but they still have a load of baby clothes to wash every day or two."

Judy passes out cards to new mothers offering to pick up, wash, and fold baby clothes. She found her first customers at the laundromat. "That's the best place to pick up new customers," she declares. "You can tell by the harassed look on their faces if they will be receptive to the idea." Judy washes the clothes at home in her family washer.

What you charge for this service depends upon what people are willing to pay or can afford. In more affluent neighborhoods you can get more.

Diapers should be rinsed well before washing, preferably in mild vinegar water, then washed on the hottest setting with mild soap and borax. If you have a clothesline, line-dry them and earn more. Sunshine is good for diapers.

TYPING—Are you an accurate and reasonably fast typist? You can earn money typing. All you need is a good typewriter.

Sixteen-year-old Soo-Lin types term papers for fellow students. They get better grades for typed papers and she gets 25¢ per page.

Allyson types manuscripts for an author. Because she must turn out a perfect copy, she charges 40¢ per 250-word page, plus 10¢ for each carbon page.

Many students can't type and some authors don't want to spend the time required. These are your potential customers. Place a notice on your school bulletin board, or if you live in a college town, in the student union. Give your rates and telephone number.

Typists are usually paid a flat fee for each page or for each 1000 words. Charge more if you have to make carbon copies. Customers should furnish their own paper and carbon and should deliver their handwritten drafts to you and pick up the typed copies, unless they are college students living in a dormitory and do not have transportation.

If you plan to type term papers or theses, consult a good book which will give you the correct form for footnotes, bibliography, and punctuation. You should not be expected to correct grammatical errors. Use "liquid paper" correction fluid to make corrections and turn out the best copy you can.

FLOATING SOCIAL SECRETARIES—Many young people have earned money doing part-time social secretary work. Paula writes letters for elderly people in her neighborhood who cannot see well enough to write or whose hands are too crippled by arthritis. She also reads letters for those who cannot see.

Mona operates an answering service for neighbors who run businesses from their homes. When they are gone, calls are transferred to Mona's number. Mona keeps a log of all calls received and is paid by the number of calls received.

Laura addresses wedding invitations. If you have good penmanship, this is a possible way to earn some money. Many brides-to-be and their mothers are pleased to find someone who can relieve them of this time-consuming chore at this busy time.

Laura watches the papers for engagement anouncements and takes a handwritten note to newly engaged girls offering her services. She gives her fee, name, and telephone number.

Laura charges 3¢ for each envelope addresed. If she stuffs and stamps the envelopes too, she gets 6¢. Most of her customers have her address the envelopes in their homes. Laura used a good pen with black ink.

How to get started as a social secretary

1. If your skills fit into the social-secretary category, look around. You will find many people willing to pay for what they consider a tedious task.

2. Make a list of things you have heard adults grumble about. Make another list of things you can do well. Fit the lists together and you have a place to start.

3. You can offer services to just one individual, or advertise and provide services to many customers.

4. Always list the type of service you provide when you advertise.

GIFT WRAPPING

To fourteen-year-old Nancy, the best part of Christmas is turning drab boxes into beautifully wrapped gifts. When she learned that there were many people in her community who either don't like to wrap gifts or don't have time to do it, she decided to do something about it. She tied her need for extra Christmas money to their need to have someone else wrap their gifts.

She spreads the word around her neighborhood that she will wrap any package for anyone for a fee—so much per package with a discount for several done at one time. Her customers have a choice of supplying paper and ribbons or paying extra for these.

"Sometimes I get some really weird things to wrap," Nancy says. "Once I had to wrap a 3-foot plant stand. I put it in a dark green trash bag and tied it with a red ribbon. Fortunately my customer was delighted."

If you like to gift-wrap, let people know you are good at it. It is better to do the wrapping in their homes; then the customers can be certain there will be no mixup.

If you are really good at wrapping packages, there is a chance to earn extra money during holiday sales in small shops. Offer to gift-wrap in the store for a commission—that is, for so much per package. That way the shop won't lose money, and you earn some. The shop will attract more customers because it offers this extra service. Many small shops don't hire regular gift wrappers, but could use someone at Christmas, Mother's Day, or graduation time. Agree to come in for an hour or two each afternoon after school or two or three times a week, or whatever is needed.

WAITERS' CLUB—If you live in a town where there are no waiters' unions, this is a good way for a group to earn money. Here's how it works. Five to ten boys and girls join together to wait on tables for dinners and banquets catered for civic organizations.

One group of boys makes up cards advertising their services and gives them to every caterer in their town. They charge a flat fee per waiter for each meal they serve, plus their own meals.

One boy acts as chairman for the group. His name and telephone number is listed on the cards. When a call comes in, he in turn calls the required number of boys to serve. They rotate so that everyone has an equal chance. If one can't work the night he is called, he passes his turn on to the next boy in line.

If you are interested in this kind of work, get a group of friends together and talk to several caterers. Ask them to try you at a reduced fee. Agree to serve tables only. Charge extra if you are expected to wash dishes. A uniform of some kind is

a nice touch. These boys wear black trousers, white shirts, red vests, and black bow ties.

MOVING—Five teen-agers jumped at the opportunity to be helpful and earn some extra money when they learned that a bookstore was moving into a larger shop. They asked the manager to hire them to help her move. These boys and girls boxed books in the old store and then placed them on the shelves in the new store. The manager was pleased with the arrangement because the young people worked hard and did a good job, and because it cost her much less than a professional mover would have.

Most stores place an announcement in the paper when they are going to move to a new location. If it is a store that handles large quantities of small items such as a bookstore, drugstore, or shoe store, ask the manager if he or she could use your help.

Antique shops and used furniture stores move large numbers of items. If you are sixteen or older, check with a local shop. They might hire you to help.

5

Pets and Plants Pay

Almost everyone has a pet or a plant and will pay good money for their care. If you love plants and animals, you can earn some of that money by offering to take care of them. There is no better way to earn money than doing something you enjoy.

Here are six ways others have done it.

DOG ESCORTING—Lots of kids walk dogs or care for them while their owners are on vacation. Twelve-year-old Jerry runs a dog escort service in his apartment building. He has five regular customers, but takes only one dog at a time for a 15-minute run around the block each evening after dinner. He gets paid 25¢ per dog to do this. He carries a plastic bucket with a lid, and a sandbox shovel and rake. When the dog makes a pile, Jerry scoops it up with the rake and shovel and deposits it in the bucket, then flushes it down the toilet when he gets home.

To get this kind of job, leave a card with your name and telephone number under the doors of apartments where you know dogs live.

PET AND PLANT SITTING—Many teen-agers "sit" for small animals such as mice, turtles, gerbils, guinea pigs, birds, or fish while friends or neighbors are on vacation. These are taken into their homes. The teen-agers charge anywhere from 25¢ a day for a mouse to $1 a day for a bird. Be sure you know how to care for any animal you agree to take.

One ten-year-old boy had the sole responsibility of feeding and watering a cat and dog for a neighbor who was gone for two months. The animals were in a fenced-in yard and the boy kept the food at his home. He fed the animals twice a day and put out fresh water daily.

If you would like to start a pet service, think up a clever way to advertise it. Hang a notice on every door in your neighborhood or apartment building. Keep your fees low. Here is how one boy's advertisement looked.

One boy bathes dogs. "Stick to the small breeds," he advises. "They are easier to manage."

Plants are much easier to sit for than animals or babies. Almost everyone has house plants. They will need attention if their owners are gone for more than a week.

If you have a "green thumb" and like tending plants, this is a good way to earn extra cash.

Let friends and neighbors know you are in the plant-sitting business. You will get a lot of business if you charge a moderate fee per plant for a week's care. You could give a discount to a customer with many plants. The customer should be responsible for bringing the plants to you and picking them up.

Tips

1. Be sure you have a suitable place with enough room and plenty of sunshine to keep plants. Some plants need full sunshine, some don't. You also need to know how much water to give them and how often.

2. Ask your customers to write down care instructions for each plant and tape the instructions to each pot. Refer to the instructions daily.

3. If you keep plants for more than one person at a time, tape the customer's name on the pots.

HORSE SITTING—Fourteen-year-old Betty has a horse-sitting business. Many boarding stables or paddocks provide pasture and shelter only. It is the responsibility of the owners to feed, groom, and exercise their own horses.

Several of Betty's friends have horses that are kept in this kind of stable. Betty wants to buy a horse of her own, so she is earning money toward that goal by feeding, combing, and exercising her friends' horses when the owners are on vacation. She also received permission to post a sign on the stable gate to let others know about her services. She earned $75 in one summer.

If you like horses and live near a stable or know boys or girls who own horses, you might try this.

HORSE EXERCISING—Ellen exercises horses for a neighbor who raises and trains horses. "I really don't like horses that much," she says, "but Mr. Grover likes the way I ride, and it is an easy way to earn money."

Not everyone is lucky enough to live near a horse trainer, but you might be hired to exercise horses at a riding stable.

One thirteen-year-old gives horses beauty treatments. She earns $5 for braiding the tails and manes of show horses. If you know how to braid and know people who like to show their horses, look into this possibility.

STABLE CLEANING—Fourteen-year-old Carole and her two brothers, Danny, 12, and Timmy, 11, are hired as a team to clean a riding stable every Saturday. For this they are paid a flat fee which they split between them.

Horse stables, dairy barns, egg factories, broiler coops, and rabbitries all require periodic cleaning. Most are located near large towns. If you can stand the stench you can earn good money this way.

Be there when you are supposed to be, and work until the job is done. Wear old clothes, of course, and wash them afterwards.

One-time possibilities for this kind of work are cleaning rodeo

grounds, race tracks, or livestock pens at fairgrounds after the fair is over. Talk to a member of the fair board about it as soon as the date for the fair, rodeo, or race is announced.

FISH FEEDING AND CAGE CLEANING—Twelve-year-old Bruce has a part-time job at a pet store. He had been a regular browser—stopping in every day on his way to school to talk to or pet the dogs, and sometimes helping feed them. When the owner's wife and partner became ill, the owner had more jobs than he could handle alone so he hired Bruce to help out. Now Bruce goes in every morning before school to feed the tropical fish and clean the bird and animal cages.

Thirteen-year-old Marsha cleans pens and feeds dogs at a boarding kennel. She used her experience as a volunteer at the SPCA to help land her job.

78

Most large cities have pet stores and boarding kennels. If you like animals, visit a kennel or pet store. Take note of the things you could do. Then talk to the manager. Point out to him how you would be good for his business. If you have had experience walking dogs or sitting for any animal, tell him about it. This will show the manager that you know how to take care of animals, and that you are dependable and reliable.

GROWING SEEDLINGS—A miniature greenhouse, given him as a gift, started twelve-year-old Glen in the seedling business. He raised his first seedlings for the family garden and gave extras to a neighbor. The neighbor was so pleased with the hardy plants that he insisted upon paying Glen for them.

Glen figured that if this neighbor was willing to pay for his plants, others would be, too. So the next year he planted twice as many seeds and sold the young plants to other gardeners in his neighborhood for less than they cost at stores or nurseries. Because the plants were strong and healthy, he sold all he had. Now he grows several boxes of flower and vegetable seedlings under fluorescent lights.

Glen buys good seed stock, but he also collects seeds from the best flowers in the neighborhood. Since his neighbors are his customers, they cooperate in saving seeds for him. He tests the seeds in a damp cloth several weeks before seeding time to be sure they will germinate.

How you can do it

If you have a "green thumb," like to grow plants, live in an area where people have garden plots or flower beds, and can plan ahead for a year or two, you might try this. You won't earn much the first year because you need to grow flower or vegetable seedlings for your own garden first, but you can sell your surplus, if any. That way you will get the hang of it and have a better idea of the amount of time and work involved. Glen says that flowers and tomatoes sell best in his neighborhood.

1. Keep your overhead low by making your own miniature greenhouse. Cut open three wire coat hangers and bend them into wickets. Make a 12 × 18-inch wooden tray 3 inches deep. Fill with rich potting soil. After the seeds have been sown and watered, poke the ends of the wickets into the soil, placing one at each end of the tray and one in the middle. Then slip the tray into a large clear plastic bag. Set in a south window. After seeds germinate, turn the tray every day to keep plants growing straight.

2. Sow your seeds in rows across the tray, 6–8 seeds per inch. Cover very lightly with soil. Water with a fine mist spray.

3. When his plants are 2 inches tall, Glen either thins them or replants them so that he has one plant for every 2 square inches. He repots the thinned plants in individual cups filled with potting soil and sets them on a cooky sheet.

"Planting seeds in peat pellets is the easiest method because they don't have to be thinned," he says, "but it increases the overhead. The pellets cost five to ten cents each."

4. Glen doesn't need to advertise, but you could place an ad in the free community bulletin or leave a sheet listing the kinds of seedlings you have for sale with their price, plus your name, address, and telephone number at the door of every neighbor who might be interested.

5. You will have no difficulty selling healthy plants if your price is lower than the market price for similar plants.

6. Keep track of your expenses. Add the cost of potting soil and fertilizer, if used. Do not spend more than you can make!

6

There's Money in Serving Small Fry

If there is one thing most teen-agers have had experience with, it is taking care of younger children. Almost everyone has baby-sat at one time or another for a younger brother or sister, or a friend or neighbor. But there are other ways of making money serving small fry. Some young people have given baby sitting a new twist. Others have made money serving tots simply by doing what they know and like to do best.

Here's how ten have done it.

BIG SISTER FOR HIRE is the way ten-year-old Kelly advertises her services. She lives in a neighborhood where there are many preschoolers and Kelly cashes in on it. If you, too, like little children, you might try this. Kelly visits the children in their homes. This gives their parents an opportunity to see how well she gets along with the little ones. Then she tells the parents she is available for hire by the hour just to play with the children in their own home, take them for walks, or accompany them to the playground. She has made up cards to give to the parents so they can call her when she is needed.

Kelly got the idea while playing with two preschool neighbors. Their mother commented that she wished they had a big sister to keep track of them while she got some work done.

Occasionally Kelly accompanies a child to a movie. Then she is paid her modest hourly fee plus her movie admission. Kelly is getting valuable experience and building up a clientele for when she's old enough to do regular baby sitting.

Mothers with more than one preschooler are most receptive to this service.

"Don't try to take more than two to the park, playground, or movies at a time," Kelly advises. "It is too hard to keep up with more than that."

You should get about half as much for doing this service as for regular baby sitting.

FREDDY'S ESCORT SERVICE—If you don't enjoy playing with preschoolers, you can provide an escort service for 5- to 8-year-olds similar to the one Freddy has. He escorts youngsters to swimming lessons, dancing lessons, music lessons, Scout activities, the skating rink, Little League practice, and the movies. If it is beyond walking or biking distance, Freddy takes them by public transportation.

This is a service any busy mother will appreciate.

BABY WALKING—Babies like a walk as much as dogs and horses do. They need the exercise and fresh air, too. The trouble is that their mothers are sometimes too tired or too busy to take them for a walk every day. That is how you can earn some pocket money.

Ten-year-old Sarah is a professional baby walker. She got her start when she heard her neighbor complain that her eighteen-

84

month-old baby wouldn't go to sleep at night without a walk around the block in his stroller. Sarah offered to take the baby for her. The grateful mother offered to pay her to do it every night.

Sarah enjoyed it so much that she offered her services to other mothers. Not all of them use her every day, but they do hire her at least once a week.

Baby walking may not seem like much of a job, but like any

other job, it gives you experience. And that will help you when you are older and apply for a bigger job. It will tell your future employer that you are responsible, reliable, and dependable—necessary qualifications for getting any job.

Pointers for baby walkers

1. Toddlers like to run free and explore. If you take an 18-month to 3-year-old child for a walk instead of a stroller ride, make it short or you may end up having to carry him or her home. Children of that age can't walk far.

2. Be sure you keep your eyes on the child every minute to keep him from darting into the street. Better still, hold his hand if he will let you.

3. Choose a route free from barking dogs. Little children are easily frightened.

4. When taking a child in a stroller, make sure he does not stand up or get his foot caught in the wheel.

5. Do not stop to chat or play with a friend. It is all right to let the friend walk along with you, if you do not forget your responsibility.

PIANO TEACHER'S BABY TENDER—Eleven-year-old Carmela earns her own spending money keeping two preschoolers quiet and out of their mother's way while she teaches piano lessons in her home. Carmela works two hours three afternoons a week. On warm days she takes the children outside to play, but on cold or wet days she reads to them or they watch television.

Many piano teachers give lessons in their homes. Some stop teaching when they have preschool-aged children, but would continue if they had someone to tend their children while they taught. That is where you come in.

If you know a music teacher or art teacher who has stopped giving lessons because she has a new baby, talk to her about this. This is a job ten- and eleven-year-olds can do because the mother is available in case of a real emergency or crisis. Point out to your prospective employer how the arrangement can be cheaper and more satisfactory for her than a day nursery.

One girl paid for her own violin lessons by sitting for her teacher during other students' lessons.

CHILD'S VACATION COMPANION—Fourteen-year-old Sue earned money and got a free vacation at the same time. She accompanied a family she baby-sits for regularly to their lake cabin as a companion to their children. Her duties included amusing the children on the long drive to and from the cabin, taking the children swimming, and caring for them while the parents fished or went out for the evening. She was paid a fee plus her lodging, meals, and transportation.

How you could get a similar job

Many families spend their vacations camping or in cabins at the lake, seashore, or mountains. Parents who like to come and go as they please and still want to feel secure in the knowledge that their children are safe with a known sitter would appreciate this service.

Talk to the families you sit for regularly or occasionally about hiring you as a companion to their children on their vacation. Or make a card something like this one, to give to each family:

> Ever need a sitter when you are on vacation?
> I am available to accompany you
> on your trip
> as a companion to your children
> June 15   through   August 15
> at $—— per week
> Plus lodging, meals, and transportation.
> I agree to keep them amused on the trip both ways
> and to sit, up to 6 hours each day, if needed.
> Sue Gilmore   Phone 444-8876

Have the card ready a few weeks before school is out. Almost everyone needs time to think about a new idea. You might be able to line up two or three jobs in a summer. You won't get rich, but you could get some great vacations.

Sue suggests that you pack a small bag with books and games suitable for the age of the children in your care, to keep them amused in the car. *Caution*—Never attempt this with anyone you do not know well or whom your parents do not approve of. Your parents may see potential problems you can't. Be businesslike. Be sure your duties are well defined before you depart. Get it in writing with both your signatures so there will be no chance of a misunderstanding.

TUTORING—If you do well in language, math, reading, spelling, history, science, or penmanship, you might try tutoring. Many teen-agers tutor younger children in school subjects they have excelled in themselves.

Fourteen-year-old Gladys tutors a little girl who has a reading problem. The child's teacher recommended that her parents drill her in reading skills every day. Since both parents work and don't have time for the additional drill periods, Gladys offered to do it for them.

Fifteen-year-old Bert tutors a ten-year-old boy in math. "I can understand it so much better when Bert explains it to me," the boy says.

Prices for tutoring vary depending upon where you live. Find out what other tutors are getting in your area. You won't be paid as much as a trained adult, but you should make anywhere from 75¢ to $2.00 per thirty-minute period. Thirty minutes is about as long as a young child can concentrate on one subject. Three sessions a week is usual.

To find customers, get permission to place a sign on the elementary school bulletin board; or if you know some of the teachers, ask them to recommend you to parents of children needing help. You could pass out cards to neighbors with school-aged children. Ask friends or parents' friends to recommend you. List your subject preferences, fees, and telephone number.

It is better to tutor in the child's home if one of his parents or another responsible adult is present. If neither will be there, do the tutoring in your home. Arrange for a quiet room where you will be uninterrupted for 30 minutes or an hour.

SUPER-BRAIN CLASS—Are you a super brain? Why not start a "Gifted Kids' Special Interest Class" for gifted children aged 7 to 10? That's what sixteen-year-old Jason did. His school system made no provisions for young gifted children. "I was just filling a need," he says.

He knew from personal experience that gifted children need an opportunity to associate with others who are gifted. He figured that most would be willing to pay a fee to explore areas not covered by the public schools. He was right. When word got around about his class, he had more applicants than he could handle.

Jason recommends that you limit your students to 5 or 6 at first, unless you have a friend to help. "If all goes well, you can add as you go along," he advises.

The number of hours or days you meet per week can be determined by the amount of time you have to spare and the interest shown by your students. If you have time and have enough applicants, have two classes.

"You will have better success if you let the students help determine the areas to explore," Jason says. Some of the subjects his classes have explored include computers, robots, and extrasensory phenomena.

How to find students

Post signs announcing your class on the grade school and library bulletin boards. Those interested will find you. Or ask teachers to give you names and addresses of students that might be interested and send them a letter.

TEACHING—If you are better than average at doing almost anything younger children like to do, from hula-hooping to yo-yoing, you have an opportunity to make money. Many enterprising young people have earned lots of dollars giving lessons to eager learners, and have found it rewarding in other ways as well.

Jennifer, a high school cheerleader, finds teaching younger children something they want to know exhilarating. She says, "I do better myself because of the extra effort I put out." The grade school children in her neighborhood used to gather around to watch the cheerleaders work out on Jennifer's front lawn. When the little girls begged to do the routines, Jennifer started a class for them.

She has 5 students who pay $1 each for an hour's instruction. "It's amazing how quickly they catch on," says Jennifer, beaming with pride. "They really are quite good."

Fifteen-year-old Kent, a Pony League pitcher, was frequently approached by Little League ballplayers for help with their pitching. In self-defense, Kent set up a class, offering to set aside one hour a week to teach anyone who paid him 75¢ a lesson. Kent's earnings average several dollars a week, and his own pitching has improved. "I guess it's because teaching makes me more aware of what I'm doing," he says.

A fifteen-year-old baton twirler, Donna, teaches twirling to 5- and 6-year-olds. They practice in her garage in cold weather and outdoors in warm weather. Her first students were neighbor children who gathered to watch her practice and asked to be shown how to do it.

Ann, a talented young ballet dancer who had been taking lessons for ten years, advertised in the community paper for her first students. Ann limits her classes of tiny tots to six, because that is all her family recreation room will accommodate. She has a long waiting list of prospective students.

Nina, 15, gives private tennis lessons to 8-to-10-year-olds. Fourteen-year-old Dorothy gives violin lessons. Ben gives drum lessons.

Although it is more fun to teach children what they want to learn and ask to be taught, there is money to be earned from teaching the many things their parents want them to learn—gymnastics, acrobatics, skating, canoeing, skiing, horseback riding, archery, sailing, golf, tap dancing, cooking, sewing, piano, and almost any other musical instrument, to name a few.

How to get started

Sit down and brainstorm the things you do well that children might like to learn.

Place an ad in a free community paper or leave flyers door to door. State your experience or qualifications as a teacher, plus your fee per lesson. Keep your classes small—children can get unruly. You can control them by telling them they can stay in the class only if they behave.

SANTA FOR HIRE—Children enjoy receiving a visit from Santa on Christmas Eve. This is an easy way to earn Christmas money.

Sixteen-year-old Scott began his job as a Santa for hire when a friend of his parents' asked him to wear a rented Santa costume and pay a visit to her children on Christmas Eve. Some of her neighbors heard about it and asked him to stop by their homes, too.

The venture was so successful that Scott decided to try it again the next year. His mother made a costume for him from red velveteen cloth and white fake fur. He bought his wig and whiskers at a costume shop.

Two weeks before Christmas he placed an ad in the paper, posted signs in the laundromat, and gave all his neighbors a card:

SANTA FOR HIRE
$3 for a 15-minute visit
Dec. 23, 24, & 25
To make reservations, call Scott
Phone 334-0798

He received so many calls that he cut future visits to 10 minutes. He made $100 in the three nights.

Scott says it's hard to tell what to expect. "You sort of have to play it by ear. Every place is different. Some people ask you to hand out gifts, some just want you to talk to the children, and others take pictures of you with the children."

Boys aren't the only ones who can play Santa. Margaret H. has been a successful Santa for several years. She advises you to be sure you have a good false beard and wig. Kids can spot a fake-looking one in a minute.

"Do wear padding. Santa is supposed to be chubby. If you

already have a Santa build like I have, you have a distinct advantage. It'd be great if you had a real Santa beard, too," she says.

In the towns where Margaret and Scott live, there is more demand for Santas than there are Santas because they can visit only a limited number of homes in a season.

Pointers for Santa

1. Let small children come to you. Many little children are frightened by Santa.

2. Don't come on too strong or overact. Play it low-key.

3. Make your exit clean and quick. Explain that you have other children to visit.

4. If there are to be a large number of children, as for a party, arrange in advance to stay longer and charge accordingly.

PARTY PLANNING—Do you like to give parties? Fifteen-year-old Beth plans birthday parties for children of working mothers, and gets paid to do it. Her services include shopping for paper plates, cups, invitations, favors, hats, balloons, and anything else her customers require.

She also bakes and decorates the cake when asked, orders the ice cream, addresses and mails the invitations, and selects games for the party or provides other types of entertainment. Sometimes her customers ask her to stay through the party to organize the games and clean up afterward. She gets paid extra for this.

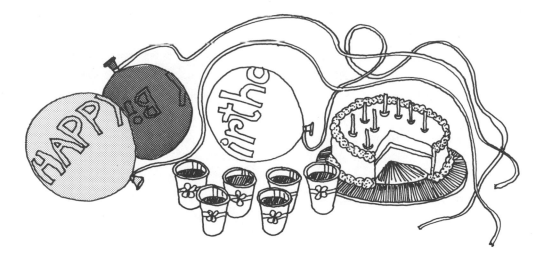

You need to be a good organizer to be a party planner. Beth collects party ideas. She goes through old magazines and clips party plans and games. She keeps these in a scrapbook.

You can be a general, all-around party planner, or you can specialize in children's birthday parties as Beth does. Or, if you prefer, you can specialize in teen-age parties, surprise parties, or holiday parties. Use your imagination. Pick what appeals to you most and have a ball earning money.

Beth got her start giving birthday parties for her younger brothers and sister, then for her neighbors' children. Her parties were so successful that she was recommended to others and soon received more requests for her services than she could fill.

Her fee varies. It is based on how long it takes her to plan the party. She gets around $10 for planning a simple two-hour party with 10 guests.

Beth recommends that you start small and build up to what you feel you can handle. As your experience grows, so will your confidence.

Pointers for party planners

1. Meet with your customer at least a week before the party to discuss all details and determine exactly what is wanted and what you are expected to do. Unless you feel really competent with food preparation, refreshments should be left up to the customer.

2. Write up your party plans, including all games, and show them to your customer at least two days before the party.

3. Your arrangement should include all costs including favors, decorations, invitations, and postage, and anything else you are expected to shop for, plus your fee. Insist upon knowing how much your customer is willing to pay. Keep within that budget even if you have to make invitations or favors rather than buy them.

4. Keep an accurate account of your expenses. Present a copy to your employer.

5. Charge more if you are expected to stay through the party. Some customers want this service; some don't.

6. On the day of the party, arrive at the house in ample time to put up decorations, set up tables and chairs, and get all materials for games in place.

7. Plan for at least 5 or 6 games, with a couple in reserve. Make games suitable for the age level.

8. Volunteer to give a party for a friend or neighbor. If it is a success, ask to be recommended to others. Advertise your services in the newspaper. Don't get discouraged if you aren't deluged with calls right away. It takes time to build a reputation and establish yourself in this sort of business. The more successful parties you plan, the more calls you will receive.

PARTY ENTERTAINERS—One thing every child has is a birthday. Birthdays mean parties, right? With so many mothers willing to pay well for party entertainment, what a rich lode of moneymaking opportunities you have! In one city a group of junior high students are mining this pay dirt. They have joined together and formed a company called Harlequin Players. They offer a package deal of 1 clown, 1 magician, and 1 puppet show to mothers who want to provide live entertainment. The entertainers charge $15 for a 1½-hour show.

Magician

Some young people prefer to go it alone. Fourteen-year-old Tony is a sleight-of-hand artist who performs magic for parties, banquets, and organizations. His first audience was children in the neighborhood who gathered around to watch him practice. After he performed for a Scout troop he was in business. Most of his calls are for kids' parties, but he prefers to perform for adults—they pay more. He doesn't need to advertise. He is good enough that his reputation keeps him busy.

If you are interested in magic, most large cities have magic shops where you can buy equipment and books on how to be a magician. Many of the shops give lessons also, but the only way you can be successful is to practice, practice, practice. One good thing about performing for little children—they are pleased with very simple tricks and short programs.

Ventriloquist

"Ryan and Friend" is how fifteen-year-old Ryan bills her ventriloquism act. Her puppet, a blond freckled boy named Teddy, was given her as a gift when she was eleven. Ventriloquism was just a fascinating pastime until a friend of her mother asked Ryan to perform at a PTA meeting. She was an instant success and received dozens of calls during the next week. Now Ryan and Teddy are frequent guests at birthday parties. She also performs at dinners and business meetings for a variety of organizations. She gets paid more for adult functions, but likes performing for children best. Teddy tells stories to the children and sings with them.

"It's fun and doesn't take up too much of my time," Ryan says, "but sometimes it's hard to keep my calls straight, especially when I get several in one week." She always gets a surge of calls right after she has appeared before an adult group.

Ryan doesn't plan to go professional. She says, "I'd rather do something else with my life, but for now it's fun and a good moneymaker."

Party clown

SILLY SIMON
CLOWN FOR HIRE
$5 for 30 minutes
Sandy Shea   933-1642

So you aren't a magician or a ventriloquist. Then be a clown. Can you think of a better way of earning money than clowning around? This is just what fifteen-year-old Sandy does. When he entertains at children's parties he does clown tricks, talks to the children, and helps open the presents. For this he gets paid $5 for a 30-minute visit!

Sandy advertised for his first customers by visiting a local playground and performing a juggling act in full costume. At the end of his act he gave cards to the children who had gathered to watch. He told them he'd come to their next birthday party if their mother would call the number on the card. He doesn't need to advertise now. He has as many calls as he can handle.

Tips for entertainers

1. Children are easily entertained, but do keep your act short and simple for tiny tots. They have a short attention span.

2. What can you do for an act? Anything children enjoy watching. Think back; it hasn't been so long since you were a little kid. What did you and your friends enjoy? Were you the classroom comedian? Then be a stand-up comedian. Are you good at telling stories, making balloon animals, performing yo-yo tricks, putting on puppet shows (with the help of friends), doing acrobatics, or telling fortunes?

One teen-ager is very successful at reading cards for older

kids and junior high parties. She got her start as a volunteer card reader at a school carnival.

3. Once you've chosen your act, practice. Practice until you are perfect. Never go commercial until you are perfect. Kids can be cruel critics.

4. Diversify. If you get too specialized, your moneymaking possibilities will be limited. Though you may find a dozen or more kids who enjoy watching a scientific demonstration, you will find many, many more who will enjoy watching you put a trained dog or bird through its paces. One boy covers two bases at once by billing himself as a clown magician.

5. Change your routine occasionally, especially if the guests are from the same neighborhood. Kids get bored when they've seen the same act over and over.

6. Make your act different from anyone else's. Use originality and come up with a gimmick that will make your act stand out among all others. Many teen-agers find it easier to perform in costume. Create a costume that can be your trademark. You needn't be a clown. You can be a storybook character such as Raggedy Ann, a pirate, a robot, or almost anything. Capitalize on the current fictional TV heroes, but don't infringe on copyrights. Wee tots love animal characters. You probably shouldn't be Mickey Mouse, but you could be his country cousin.

7. Give your character and act a clever, catchy name.

8. When you've gained experience in your neighborhood and are ready to spread out, advertise.

Performing for adult groups is the very best advertising you can get, even if you don't get paid, especially if you can get the person who introduces you to mention that you are available for kids' parties. Have cards with your name, your character's name, and your telephone number on them ready to hand out to prospective customers. One boy used a rubber stamp to make his first cards.

Place ads in the daily newspaper and free community bulletins.

Posters can be pinned up any place mothers of small children go—laundromats, grocery stores, ice cream stores, or day-care centers. One boy is listed in the yellow pages of the telephone directory under his clown name, but since this is rather expensive, it isn't recommended unless you plan to go professional.

Once you have established your reputation, word of mouth will probably get you all the business you want.

9. Keep an appointment book to record all your calls in so that you won't get mixed up and won't overbook yourself. Enter every engagement with time and place.

10. If you must provide your own transportation to and from the functions, charge extra to cover the cost.

7

Part-time Jobs

Part-time jobs are hard to find. If you are under sixteen they are practically nonexistent. Anyone who has tried to find one can tell you that. Nonetheless, many young teen-agers have obtained regular part-time jobs. They did it by using ingenuity. They saw something that they could do and because they offered to do it at a reasonable price, they were hired, even though the managers might never have hired anyone for those particular jobs before.

When approaching business people about a job, it helps if you can show how hiring you will save both money and time for the business. The trick is to offer to do the job on a contract basis. That way you can set your own pace without feeling pressured. When you do a job on a contract basis, you are paid for the job instead of by the hour; therefore you are saving your employer both time and money. He doesn't have to pay minimum wages or bother with paperwork of withholding and social security taxes. You are also saving your employer money by doing a job that usually takes a highly paid employee's time. The faster you work, the more actual hourly pay you receive.

103

Small, locally owned shops which hire few adults will offer the best opportunity for this kind of employment.

Always find out what you will be paid before you accept a job. This is the businesslike way to go about it.

BOATYARD WORKER—Boating is in sixteen-year-old Kevin's blood. He has hung around the waterfront since he was 12, often volunteering to crew; sometimes helping boat owners wash down their boats and doing small repair jobs. Now Kevin spends his days cleaning hulls and gets paid to do it. He has a summer job in a boatyard.

Kevin advises, "If you'd like to get a similar job, get out on the water. Get in contact with boats and boating people by hanging around the waterfront and volunteering to help."

If you are strong, willing to work hard, and like boats, this could be just the job for you. There is always plenty of work around a small boatyard, marina, or yacht club that needs to be done. There are many a teen-ager can do—cleaning hulls, painting bottoms, calking seams, launching boats. You might even be lucky enough to get a job as a boatboy on a yacht.

How to get a similar job

1. You need to have a basic knowledge of boats, lines, knots, hand tools, and nomenclature (the special names and terms used in marinas and boatyards).

2. You can get experience with boats as Kevin did by hanging around the boatyard, and you can help friends and neighbors work on their boats. Kevin got his job through a neighbor who was a customer at the boatyard. He put in a good word for Kevin and told him about the job opening.

You can also find many books on boating that will teach

you about basic seamanship, sailboat handling, nomenclature, knots, and lines. You can practice using hand tools and lines at home.

3. While boating experience is not absolutely necessary, the ability to work hard and seriously at a steady pace all day is.

4. Apply in person at the marina or boatyard office. State your experience, abilities, and references. Leave your name and telephone number. Marinas are located in coastal towns and on inland resort lakes. Boatyards and yacht clubs are found mostly along the seacoast, Great Lakes, or large rivers.

5. A great many people thoughout the country own small boats. These are often stored through the winter in backyards. Come spring, the owners can be seen scraping, caulking, and painting their boats. This is a good job opportunity for young people. Almost anyone would appreciate some help for this laborious task!

SHELF DUSTING—Thirteen-year-old Linda got a job as a shelf duster in a bookstore. This was a job she created for herself. When a family friend opened a bookstore, Linda volunteered to help paint the walls without pay. Then she asked about dusting the shelves after the store opened. She offered to do them for a set fee per shelf. Working 2½ hours, two days a week, she earned between $3 and $5 per week. After a time she earned extra money shelving newly arrived books.

If you are interested in this kind of work, talk to the owner of your favorite bookstore. It will help if you like books and have been a regular customer.

What other types of stores might need shelves dusted? Antiques and gifts must collect a lot of dust and it must take a lot of time keeping the shops tidy.

PHONE ANSWERING AND FLOOR SWEEPING—Some beauty salons and barbershops will employ young people on a part-time basis to answer the telephone, make appointments, and sweep up clipped hair. One girl noticed that her beauty operator spent more time answering the telephone than cutting her hair, so she suggested that the operator hire her to answer the phone. The operator liked the idea and hired her. Her job consisted of answering the telephone and sweeping up hair clippings on the three busiest summer mornings each week, and on Saturdays during the school year.

Most places of business must be swept every day. Some of the smaller places will hire a young person to do this. You will never know unless you ask.

Shop owners sometimes hire young people to keep the sidewalks in front of their stores clean. Contact the manager and ask for the job. Quote a price that will be hard to refuse. Your duties might include sweeping, digging out grass and weeds, and shoveling snow. This job could be a one-time thing, but it could also develop into a regular part-time job.

Many shop owners also hire young people to wash display windows. Sometimes they provide the squeegee mops needed. If you have your own equipment, inquire about washing windows for any small business that has large plate glass windows. Talk to the manager. If he cannot hire you, ask him if he knows anyone else who might be able to use a window washer.

OFFICE SITTING—Fifteen-year-old Doug has a job as an office sitter for a roofing company. He got the idea when his mother, who wanted someone to repair the roof, had to dial the office fifteen times before someone answered the phone.

"What that company needs is an office sitter!" declared Doug. When the contractor came to make an estimate, Doug

approached him with the idea. Doug pointed out how his services could make money for the company. It made sense to the contractor and he agreed to try it out. Now he says Doug is definitely an asset to the company because they do not lose customers because of missed calls.

Doug likes being an office sitter. "It makes me feel important because I know I am really contributing something to the company," he says. "I don't have time to get bored because the phone rings about every fifteen minutes."

Besides answering the phone, Doug keeps the office clean and does other little jobs for his boss. When he has nothing else to do, he reads. Doug offers these basic rules for answering the telephone:

1. Be courteous, even when the customer isn't.

2. Answer with the business firm's name.

3. *Always* take the name, number, and address of the person calling.

4. Take good notes. Write down everything the customer says. Don't trust to memory. You might get fifteen calls in a single morning. You can't possibly keep them all separate in your mind.

5. Assure the customers that your boss will call them back at a stated time. Doug's boss returns calls during his noon hour and after five.

6. *Always* remember to deliver messages.

Doug fills an important need. Any small company that depends upon telephone calls for its business and whose owner must be out of the office a great part of the day can use an office sitter. Small construction contractors, building contractors, plumbers, electricians, excavators, window washers, some kinds of salesmen, and repairmen are a few such companies.

Do you know any insurance salesmen, lawyers, vacuum cleaner salesmen, or realtors who are brown-bagging it because they don't want to miss a client's phone call? They could use a noon-hour office sitter. Young lawyers just getting established dislike closing the office even for an hour at noon lest they miss a prospective client's call.

A live voice on the phone is much better for any business than a tape-recorded message. That's why Cecilia's services are well received. She office-sits for professionals while their secretaries are on vacation or on sick leave.

Small companies that work out of homes might be interested in hiring someone for a couple of hours to give the wife a chance to get out occasionally.

If you are an accurate typist and have taken a course in bookkeeping or office practice, you can add these skills to your office sitting. Many small businesses cannot afford to hire a full-time secretary, bookkeeper, or file clerk. Smaller cities don't usually have secretarial service companies that can be hired to do small office chores. That is where you can fill a need. Even in large cities you can get a job if your fee is smaller than those charged by the secretarial service companies.

OFFICE SITTER FOR HIRE BY THE JOB
OR BY THE HOUR
Will type, do simple bookkeeping, and filing.
No job too small.
Janette Johnson   567-9678

This is the message Janette placed in her free community bulletin and on the cards she left at small businesses such as insurance offices, realtors, craft shops, and bait suppliers. Most of her jobs come from the small businesses, but occasionally individuals hire her for typing business letters or resumés. Sometimes she is hired to sit in a one-person office to answer the telephone when the boss is away.

SILVER POLISHING—Have you ever polished silver? Fifteen-year-old Kathy polishes silver in a jewelry store. The manager offered her the job when he overheard her comment to her mother that it must take an awful lot of time to keep the hollowware polished.

Thinking he was joking, Kathy laughed and said, "Sure, how much will you pay me?"

He named a figure she couldn't refuse, and she began her new job the next day.

If this kind of work appeals to you, ask your jewelry store manager if he would be interested in hiring you to polish the silver and keep the crystal sparkling in his store. Offer to do it on a contract basis at a reasonable price, and chances are he will accept your offer. It will cost him less than having his adult clerks, who are paid by the hour, do this time-consuming work.

A word of warning: This is no job for a klutz or accident-prone person.

SHELF STOCKING—Everyone knows that grocery stores use shelf stockers. They probably also know that there are many applicants for every available job. The only way to land one of these jobs is to keep going back, "Until they hire you to get you off their backs," as one boy put it. Some teen-agers have found a better solution. They put their minds to work and thought of other stores that could use the same kind of service.

Fifteen-year-old Derek works for a self-service shoe store.

He maintains the racks, keeping them neat and making sure all sizes are in their proper places. He also restocks the shelves when new orders come in, after he has priced and stamped each shoe with the store code. His is a year-round job. He works three hours on school days and five on Saturday.

Fourteen-year-old Mario stocks shelves in an auto-parts store. He reports to work every day after school and every Saturday morning. His job consists of bringing stock from the supply room and keeping display shelves and bins full.

Have you ever gone into a music store and found the sheet music or records mixed up and out of order? Thirteen-year-old Juanita has. That's how she got her job keeping the sheet music and record bins properly filed and filled. Working two hours, three days a week, she earns enough to keep herself in spending money and puts a little away each month toward her college fund.

Many other places of business can use extra hands for restocking shelves. This is a good part-time job for you. It is something that needs doing that the regular clerks don't always have time for. Look for places with only one clerk or checkout person on duty during busy periods. Twenty-four-hour convenience stores, craft and hobby stores, small hardware or drug stores, and art supply stores are other good places to try.

LUMBERYARD LARRY—Fifteen-year-old Larry's job at a lumberyard was the result of having to stand around for 25 minutes until his father was waited on by the only salesperson in the lumberyard. "If it takes that long to take care of customers, they need more help," he reasoned. So he talked to the manager about hiring him as an "odd-jobs boy." He pointed out all the kinds of things he could do for the company and

suggested that the manager hire him for a week on a trial basis. The manager liked his idea and hired him. Larry works 4 hours a day, 5 days a week and 8 hours on Saturday. Most of Larry's work is inside. He shovels sand, mixes paint, restocks displays, carries messages, and waits on customers when no other salesperson is available. He can't work in the yard loading lumber until he is 18.

Lumberyards pay well. Some hire only people over 18, but others hire younger teen-agers. The only way to find out is to talk to the manager.

A good strategy is to pick a busy season or period of the day. Observe the routine and make a mental note of all the things you could do that would free older, more experienced sales clerks to wait on customers. Have these clearly in mind before you talk to the manager about hiring you.

For example, this is how Larry opened his interview, "Looks like you need some extra help around here. I'm just the guy who can do it. I could run errands, fetch from the stock room, carry heavy purchases to the customer's car, mix paint, restock the displays, and sack nails. And I can work only during your peak periods, saving you money during the slow time."

Employers like to hire people who can see what needs to be done and have the initiative to go ahead and do it without having to be told.

BED MAKING—Fifteen-year-old Beth does nothing but make beds in a nursing home. This frees trained aides to take care of other patient needs during the summer when the staff is reduced because of vacation schedules. This is a job Beth created for herself.

She was visiting her grandmother in the nursing home one afternoon and saw that the aides were still making beds, and giving baths, and grumbling about the extra load of work caused by vacationing aides. Beth immediately recognized an employment possibility and asked to talk to the manager.

She suggested that the manager hire her to make beds during the summer to relieve the load on the aides. She explained that she was a Candy Striper and had learned to make beds the approved hospital way. She also appreciated the necessity of wrinkle-free beds because she had spent several weeks in bed once due to an injury.

Her proposal made sense to the manager and she was hired to work four hours a day, five days a week.

114

Other teen-agers have gotten summer jobs as bed makers in busy motels in tourist areas.

EXTRA SERVICE PEOPLE—You can get part-time employment by pointing out to the manager of a business how hiring you will bring him or her more customers.

Delivery Service—For example, many places of business attract more customers if they offer a delivery service. If you own a bike, offer to deliver small items for small businesses in your neighborhood that do not already offer this service. Florists, bakeries, pizza parlors, and drug stores often need delivery service.

Car Wash Extra—Matt, 13, talked the manager of a car wash into hiring him to polish cars and vacuum the insides for customers by making a case that this extra service would attract more customers.

Here are Matt's arguments:

Although some people prefer to do this themselves, many others would rather hire it done. These are the people who will be attracted by the extra service.

8

Apprenticeships and Subcontractors

A good way to earn money and learn a trade at the same time is to become an apprentice to a trade person during the summer. If you work consistently in the same trade, by the time you are 18 you could be a journeyman and earn a good salary.

Check in your area with people in the manual trades. Many of them hire apprentices during the summer. Look also into subcontracting from older brothers and sisters or friends who have summer jobs. You can substitute for them on days they can't work.

This is the way some teen-agers have done it.

BUILDING CONTRACTOR'S APPRENTICE—Fifteen-year-old Todd's best friend worked as an apprentice carpenter for his father each summer. Todd figured that if one contractor could use an apprentice, others probably could too. Since he had nothing to lose by trying, he decided to drop by the offices of the other contractors in his town. He started early in April, arriving at their offices before eight in the morning.

"They were really impressed by my getting there so early,"

he says. "They thought I was an eager beaver, but I was really trying to catch them in the office. I had to be in school by nine and they weren't around after school."

Todd explained that he was willing to start from the ground up to learn the trade. And that is exactly where he started for the contractor who hired him. He was put to work picking up and stacking scrap pieces of lumber, dropped nails, and the like, but soon graduated to more sophisticated jobs.

"I guess they liked my work. They invited me to come back to work for them next summer," he says.

Todd worked for a building contractor. Many building sub-contractors also hire apprentice workers. Terry works as an apprentice for a non-union bricklayer. He hauls sand, carries bricks and mortar, and sometimes mixes mortar.

Plumbers, roofers, and cabinetmakers are other people to try.

APPRENTICE HOUSE PAINTER—Fifteen-year-old Mark is learning the painting business from the ground up. That means he lays the drop cloths, carries the ladder, mixes or stirs paint, cleans brushes and rollers, loads and unloads the truck, runs errands, and does any other little task that comes along. He even paints occasionally.

Mark works for the painting contractor who painted his parents' house. He made himself so helpful during the painting of their house that the contractor offered him a job for the summer.

"I'm not getting rich doing this," says Mark, "but I'm doing as well as I could at anything else and I'm sure learning a lot. Next summer I'll get a raise because I will have had experience. It beats sitting around doing nothing a long way."

118

TREE SURGEON ASSISTANT—Fourteen-year-old Pablo has a summer job as an assistant tree surgeon. Pablo got his job because he helped the tree surgeon, Mr. Platt, load the limbs from a neighbor's trees into the company truck. Mr. Platt told him he was such a good worker he could go to work for him any time. Pablo accepted the offer, and now whenever Mr. Platt has a pruning, topping, trimming, or removal job, he calls Pablo to load the lopped limbs and help haul them to the dump.

To get a similar job, stop by a tree surgeon's place of business early in the spring—late February or March would not be too soon. Offer to go with him on his next Saturday pruning job to show him what you can do. If you work hard, do a good job, and don't waste time, chances are that you will get the job, especially if you ask to be paid by the job rather than by the hour. You will be saving the tree surgeon time. And time is money in his line of work.

SALVAGE ASSISTANT—Most auto salvage yards can use cheap labor to help take apart old and wrecked cars, clean up pieces already removed, or sort and box the pieces.

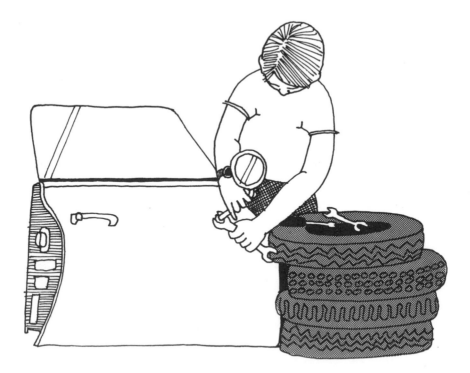

Fifteen-year-old Bill does this five mornings a week through the summer and every Saturday morning during the school year. "It is hard and dirty work," he says, "but it is worth it. I get paid, plus I get first choice at all the parts I need for my car." Bill is rebuilding a 1958 Ford.

Some salvage yards are family-owned industries and the children are put to work helping. However, not all owners have children. If they need help, they must hire it. Stop by the auto salvage yards in your area. If they seem short-handed (you can tell by the small number of used parts on display), bring to the operator's attention the ways it would be good for his business to hire you. Many of these places are owned and operated by one man who doesn't have time to disassemble many automobiles. This cuts down on his overhead, but it also cuts down on customers because they must find and remove their own pieces from the cars in his yard.

If the owner can pay you for doing a specific job, instead of by the hour, he can increase the number of pieces in his stock room at a low cost and not have to worry about paperwork connected with hiring you.

SUMMER SUBSTITUTES—Regularly employed older teens must skip family vacation trips or run the risk of losing their summer jobs, unless they can find a substitute to fill in for them while they are gone. This gives many younger teens an opportunity to earn some cash.

One twelve-year-old boy earned $50 in two weeks delivering the morning newspaper for a friend on vacation. Another twelve-year-old took over an older boy's lawn-mowing jobs while he was gone. In each case both parties benefited. The older boys didn't lose their jobs and the younger boys earned extra spending money as well as experience.

Fourteen-to-sixteen-year-olds can subcontract for many other types of jobs from older teens, providing their employers okay the arrangement. Ticket takers or helpers at refreshment stands in movie houses, ushers, car hops, servers in fast-food restaurants, and baggers at grocery stores are some of the jobs for which you could substitute.

Ask your older friends if they will need a substitute, and ask them to consider you for the job. Get a firm commitment. Don't let them keep you dangling, uncertain whether they will let you take their place.

9

Mind Your Own Business

Many young people have found a way to make money by going into business for themselves. This requires a capital investment, or money to buy supplies and equipment. In other words, they use money to make more money. Some saved their capital from their allowances. Some borrowed it from their parents. Others worked free to get their raw materials.

Going into business for yourself can be tricky, but properly managed, it can bring in a good income. Remember to keep your investment and overhead low. Overhead is the money it costs to produce your product. If raw materials, tools, and energy cost $4.75 and you sell your product for $5.00, you haven't made enough profit. Profit is the money you have left over after all expenses have been paid. You need to make at least a 20% profit to stay in business.

When considering a business of your own, look for one that has low-cost raw materials (free is best, of course), takes few expensive tools, and has a product that can be sold at a reasonably high profit. Also be sure to choose a product or service for which there is a market. Remember that unless your product cannot be bought anywhere else, you will be more suc-

cessful if people can buy it from you for less than they can elsewhere.

Be sure to check local and state laws concerning the sale of your product. Some young people have created real headaches for themselves because they didn't check these out.

For example, you may need a tax number. Call your state tax office to find out and request a number. You also need to find out about zoning laws. Some places will not allow a business to be operated in a home. If you plan to sell door to door, you may need a license. Check with your local Chamber of Commerce for answers to these questions. For a one-time sale, you probably won't need any of these.

An excellent way to learn the ins and outs of running a business is by joining a national youth organization called Junior Achievement. It is open to all junior and senior high school students. Members form companies to manufacture products which they sell, or offer services. Workers are paid a small salary and all profits are divided among the members. You can therefore earn while you learn. You can call your local chapter for more information about joining. It is listed in the telephone directory.

How to get financing

1. The best method is to save the money you will need from other earnings or from your allowance. Some teen-agers borrow money from parents, grandparents, or an older brother or sister.

2. When asking for a loan, present your moneymaking idea to the person you want to borrow money from. If that person thinks it is too risky, listen to his (or her) arguments. He has had more experience than you. If you still think your idea is good and will work, gather more information and approach someone else. Explain exactly how and why you think it will work. If more than one person considers it too risky, either wait until you have saved enough money to try it on your own or think up a new idea.

3. When you borrow money to finance a business, remember that it must be paid back. In figuring your overhead costs so that you can determine the amount of profit you will receive, don't forget to include the monthly payments on your loan.

MAIL ORDER BUSINESS—A wholesale catalog given three young brothers by a friend launched them into a booming mail-order business. They started out building skateboards for themselves from parts ordered through the catalog. When their friends began asking the boys to order boards, trucks, and wheels for them, the youths obtained a sales tax number from their state tax office and organized their firm, M & R Skateboards. With money borrowed from their mother, they expanded their business and began custom-building skateboards also. The boys sell their products 15 to 20 percent below retail prices and still have a good margin of profit because they operate out of their home basement. Their monthly earnings average about $600.

The boys advise you to do accurate bookkeeping and keep a tight inventory list. An inventory list is a detailed list of every piece of equipment you have on hand. They didn't at first, and it caused them a lot of trouble. "If you don't know how, get some responsible person—your mother, father, or an older brother or sister—to show you," suggests Randy.

If you have a sport or hobby which requires a lot of parts or other equipment to maintain, and if you know many other people interested in the same thing, you have a good opportunity for beginning a mail-order business. You need to be familiar with it to know what equipment will be needed and which is the best.

126

Other products that would make good wholesale ventures are bicycle or motorcycle parts, model railroad pieces, radios and radio parts, CB's, stereo equipment, tape-recording equipment, printing presses and paraphernalia, and camera and photographic equipment.

You can obtain wholesale catalogs from companies by writing and asking for them. Check the current *Standard Directory of Advertisers* at your public library for companies that distribute the product you need. You also can check the *Thomas Register of American Manufacturers* for the names of companies that manufacture the product. Write the manufacturer and ask for the name and address of the distributor nearest you. You can also find the names of distributors from ads in trade magazines or papers.

It helps to know an established dealer. If your mail-order business is connected with your own hobby or interest, you probably already know at least one dealer. One boy who was a frequent customer of a radio parts place used names and addresses he found in one of their trade magazines to order catalogs.

Tips for mail-order businesses

1. Unless you are completely familiar with all angles of your hobby or sport, this is not a business you should try. It is not something to go into cold. You need to know everything about your product and the demand for it.

2. You also need to know about the companies that supply your product. There may be more than one wholesale company which handles the parts or equipment you need. Get catalogs from two or more of them. Order parts for your personal use from each. This will show you which companies respond quickest and are the most reliable. After several months

127

of personal experience with them you will also learn how much time is required to receive ordered parts.

3. Type your letter when writing for a catalog (and always make a carbon copy to keep for your records). It should be typed on letterhead stationery. That is stationery that has the name and address of your company at the top. Distributors seldom send catalogs to private individuals.

4. You can make some fairly inexpensive letterhead stationery by drawing the letterhead with felt-tipped pens and having a hundred pages printed at a quick-copy shop. You will use the extra sheets for your business later.

5. When you know your companies well, you are ready to order for customers. To avoid the need for large sums of capital, let customers make their selections from your catalog and special-order the parts for them. Some businesses require customers to pay the full price at the time the order is placed. This is probably the best policy for beginners. They avoid having their own money tied up in ordered merchandise. They also avoid getting stuck with something if a customer changes his mind.

6. When you have accumulated operating capital you can order samples to show or build up a small inventory of parts most frequently ordered. Keep an accurate inventory of all equipment in stock. Avoid getting too large an inventory.

7. When placing an order, you will have to send payment with it. Therefore it is best to open a bank account so you can send checks. Cash is too risky and money orders are expensive.

8. Your customers will pay you the list or retail price (unless you offer a small discount). You will pay wholesale price to the distributor plus shipping charges. The retail price is always higher than the wholesale price. The difference between them is what you earn, your profit.

9. Even if your customer pays when ordering, do not spend your profit until he has picked up the item. If he is dissatisfied, you will have to refund his money.

10. Keep complete and accurate records. You will need at least two sets of records. First you must keep a detailed account of each order. Carbon copies are important, but you should also enter in a ledger the name and telephone number of each person making an order, the parts ordered, the company ordered from, the amount of money paid, and the date the order was made. This is your operating record.

11. You will also need a record of all your expenditures including license if needed, stationery, shipping costs, postage, and any other business expense you might have. Your record will also include all the money you collect. This is the only way to avoid spending more money than you make.

12. If you have trouble keeping all these records straight, get an older person who has had experience, preferably a parent, to show you how or do it for you.

13. Giving a small discount will increase your volume of business, but be sure you allow for your overhead. At first glance it may seem that getting a 50 percent markup on a product is a good way to get rich quick. But don't forget that you pay postage for the order and shipping costs, which can be pretty expensive. That is why it is good business to combine orders whenever you can. Order from the nearest distributor when possible. This saves on shipping costs and usually saves time.

LAWN MOWER AND BIKE REPAIR SHOP—Lawn mowing was the way fifteen-year-old Jeff earned money, until his lawn-mower repair bills grew to be more than he was making mowing. Then he decided to learn to repair the machine himself. He enrolled in a lawn-mower repair class offered at the local technical school. He did so well that he gave up mowing lawns and set up a repair service in his family garage. "That's the best fifteen dollars I ever spent," he says.

Jeff used his father's tools until he had earned enough to buy his own. With his first profits he added a flywheel holder and a flywheel puller to make his work easier.

Jeff makes a list of repair services and their cost, based on the time it takes him to do them. He leaves a list door to door. He also advertises in the community shoppers' guide.

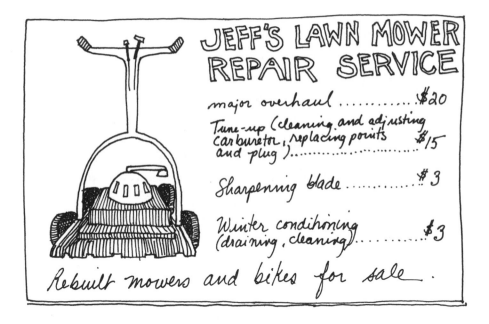

JEFF'S LAWN MOWER REPAIR SERVICE

major overhaul $20
Tune-up (cleaning and adjusting carburetor, replacing points and plug) $15
Sharpening blade $3
Winter conditioning (draining, cleaning) $3
Rebuilt mowers and bikes for sale.

If new parts are needed, Jeff buys them and adds the cost to the bill. He staples the sales slip for the part to the customer's bill.

Jeff also buys old lawn mowers from junkyards and garage

130

sales and rebuilds them. He takes usable parts from one to rebuild others. His rebuilt mowers sell for a reasonably low figure. "Most of them are almost as good as a new one. Some of my customers can't afford new mowers, especially the kids just starting a lawn-cutting service," he says.

Many of the places where he buys old lawn mowers also have broken bicycles and tricycles. Since they cost very little, Jeff buys and rebuilds these too. He uses spare parts from one bike to rebuild two or three others. He puts them in working order and when painted, they look almost as good as new. He has no trouble selling them.

How you can do it

1. A variety of repair classes are offered by many technical schools and shop classes in high school. Take advantage of these. If you are good at working with your hands and are mechanically inclined, this can be a profitable business, even if you don't want to make a career of it.

2. For a dollar or two, you can often find items that need repair, such as small appliances, bicycles, tricycles, or other pieces of equipment at garage sales, rummage sales, junkyards, or thrift shops. Many people throw away broken appliances and other items. Ask them to save these items for you.

3. While you are learning your trade, buy several and repair them. Use parts from one to repair or rebuild others.

4. Sell your rebuilt items for a profit. Advertise them in the free community paper or hold a garage sale.

5. When you have gained experience rebuilding and repairing, advertise your repair service. If you keep your prices reasonable, you will soon have plenty of customers.

6. You can send for a parts catalog from a distributor and buy repair parts wholesale. Look under the section on Mail Order Business to learn how to get a catalog.

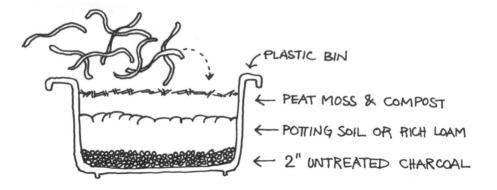

PLASTIC BIN

← PEAT MOSS & COMPOST

← POTTING SOIL OR RICH LOAM

← 2" UNTREATED CHARCOAL

WORM FARMER—If you don't need money in a hurry and have contact with many freshwater fishermen, this is a good business venture. Your initial investment is small, and worms don't eat much, don't take much care, and can be raised either indoors or outdoors.

Fourteen-year-old Ruth raises earthworms in her bedroom. She got into the business when she heard a family friend complain to her father about the shortage of fishing worms in their area. "I'd pay a dollar a dozen for good worms," he had said.

Ruth reasoned that if he'd pay that much, chances were that other fishing enthusiasts would too. She spent $10 to buy 4 dozen worms for "seed" and a plastic tub and bedding mix to put them in. Then she waited. A year later, she had an estimated 100,000 worms in 4 tubs and $500 in the bank.

How to be a worm farmer

1. Red wigglers are the easiest to raise and reproduce most rapidly. Each worm lays about 28 eggs which hatch and reach maturity within three months. Ordinary garden earthworms reproduce too slowly to be profitable.

2. Wigglers can be bought at bait shops, sporting-goods stores, or from another worm farm for less than a dollar a dozen. For fast returns, buy only mature worms. They will have distinct bands; immature worms do not.

3. Take into consideration your storage space before buying. A bin 15 × 20 × 10 inches will accommodate up to 200 worms. But they will become overcrowded and have to be divided every three months. In six months you will have 8 bins full, unless you are selling the worms rapidly. Some bins can be stacked to take less room. You could use larger bins or fewer worms to start.

4. *Culture bins*—Do not use metal tubs—some metals kill worms. Either plastic or wooden tubs make good indoor bins. You can build 15 × 20 × 10-inch wooden bins. These are easily handled and stacked. But make sure you fit seams tightly to prevent worms escaping. Outdoor bins can be larger. A garage or sheltered patio area makes a good place for worm bins. Worms must not be allowed to get colder than 40 degrees. Freezing kills them. And never put them in direct sunshine.

5. *Bedding mix*—Before filling her tubs with bedding mix, Ruth puts 2 inches of untreated charcoal in the bottom of the bins to keep them smelling sweet. She buys the charcoal at a garden and flower supply shop. For her bedding mix, she fills the box half full with rich loam or potting soil. Then she mixes equal amounts of peat moss and compost together and pours this over the loam to within 2 inches of the top.

If you have outdoor bins, mix in a sack of aged steer or rabbit manure. Manure is good worm food. Keep your worm garden moist but not wet. If it gets too wet, the worms will drown. Cover the bins with cardboard or plywood to keep the worm garden from drying out. Ruth stacks her tubs and places a round plywood disk over the top which she then covers with a round tablecloth. "It blends in with my décor and no one need know I have worms in my room," she says.

6. *Feeding and maintenance*—Grass trimmings, kitchen wastes including bacon grease, alfalfa meal, soybean meal, cottonseed meal, or corn meal are basic worm foods. "My worms love cardboard. I tear it into tiny pieces for them. And I give them old coffee grounds and tea leaves as a special treat," Ruth says. She feeds them about 1 pound of food every two weeks. Except for checking for dampness, this is all the care needed until it is time to divide the bin.

7. To determine whether your worms are producing other worms, turn over some of the soil and look for smaller worms. There should be at least as many smaller ones as big ones. Don't disturb them too often.

8. *Selling the worms*—Two or three days before she is ready to sell, Ruth transfers the worms she will sell to a tub full of pure peat moss. She adds a little meal to fatten the worms and enough water to keep them moist. "This makes the worms more transparent, tougher, and livelier," she says.

She packs the worms in cottage cheese cartons and other throwaway containers filled with dampened peat moss to sell to customers.

Ruth sells to individual sportsmen and women who come to her, but she also plans to start dealing with bait shops now that her stock has grown so large. The bait shops will furnish the packing boxes and peat moss. She expects to market 9 months out of the year.

9. *Advertising*—At first Ruth advertised only by word of mouth. She says that is still the best advertising, but she also places ads in community papers and she has a sign in front of her house. She plans to put a large ad in the daily newspaper at the beginning of each fishing season.

Tips to remember

1. Start with the largest bin you have room for and can afford. The larger your bin, the sooner you will have enough worms to harvest.

2. Keep your initial investment low so that a disaster will not cause you to lose too much.

3. To figure your initial investment, add the cost of the worms, potting soil, peat moss, compost (unless you make your own), charcoal, and your alfalfa, soybean, or corn meal. Cost will vary according to the size of your worm garden.

4. If you stock your bin with the maximum number of worms, you will need to divide it every three months or sell the excess. Keep this in mind if space is limited. There is not much market for worms during the winter in northern states.

5. *Warning:* Do not deal with "buy back firms." In spite of their claims, the only reliable market for worms at the present time is for fish bait.

6. Garages and basements are the best places to raise worms. Not many parents are as tolerant as Ruth's are.

FISH BAIT SUPPLIER—Fifteen-year-old Louis has a booming bait business. He sells sandworms and minnows to bait shops in his area. His profit is high and his overhead is low because he gets his raw material from the ocean. His only tools are a hoe, a net, and a minnow trap. He digs sandworms from the shore mud at low tide and catches minnows along the reef near the shore. On a good day he earns $20.

Louis's recommendations

1. Before you go into this business, visit two or three bait shops in your area. Get a commitment from them to buy either a minimum number of worms or minnows per week, or all you can supply. Otherwise you might end up with 500 sandworms, a bucketful of minnows, and no market.

2. Deliver the sandworms as soon after digging as possible to ensure freshness.

3. Ask the bait shop managers which days are best for delivery.

If you live inland near lakes, consider supplying the kinds of fish bait that are popular in your area. Minnows, grasshoppers, night crawlers, crickets, and crayfish are all popular. If you have a good source of raw material, talk to bait shops or sporting goods stores to see whether they are interested in buying your bait.

One boy catches grasshoppers by walking through fields of tall grass or weeds where grasshoppers are plentiful. He uses a net to catch them and usually gets a full net with a few swipes.

OTHER RICHES FROM THE SEA—The sea has provided a living for people throughout history. If you live near the shore, try to come up with new and different ways to use the sea's treasures. Lots of other young teen-agers are earning spending money this way.

Twelve-year-old Georgina catches small fish and snails from under rocks and ledges and sells them to an aquarium shop. She also collects shells to sell to tourist gift shops. If you want to try this, talk to the aquarium shops in your area to see if they will buy from you before you go fishing. A boy in Florida catches small shore fish which he sells to an aquarium to be used as food for their sea animals.

Twelve-year-old Bernie is a licensed lobster fisherman. He started three years ago with 1 trap. He now has his own boat

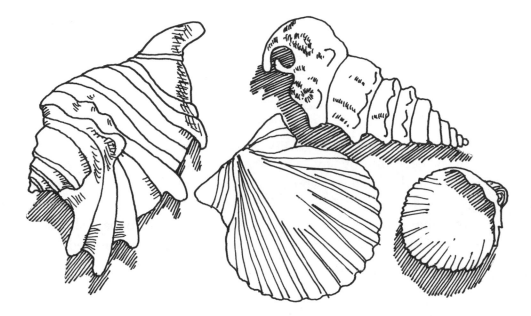

and 15 lobster traps. He hopes to double the number of traps by next year.

A boy in Maine goes "mossing" for sea moss which grows in tidal areas. IIe rakes the moss into his rowboat, then sells it to fishermen who resell it to gelatin factories. "They make Jello out of it," he says.

Many people earn pocket money beachcombing. Most look for driftwood, seashells, fossil rocks, and bottles. Fourteen-year-old Boris looks for agates along the coast of Northern Oregon. He can be seen searching along the gravel bars when the tide goes out for the semiprecious stones, which are worth several dollars. Although Boris would receive more money for the stones if he polished and mounted them, he prefers to sell unpolished stones to a dealer. "I'd rather spend my time along the shore looking for them," he says. "I'd get more for a finished piece, *if* I could sell it. But this way I have a sure market for every stone I find."

ORGANIC FERTILIZER FIRMS—Two teen-age boys found a cave which had a layer of bat droppings covering the floor. They bagged the droppings and sold it as fertilizer.

Another group of boys and girls clean a horse stable once a week for the manure which they bag and sell to gardeners, door to door.

Animal manure is one of the best all-around garden fertilizers, and there is a good market for it in most areas.

If you live within biking distances of a horse stable, chicken factory, rabbitry, sheep farm, or dairy farm, you can get into the organic fertilizer business. Manure accumulates so rapidly that most farmers can't use all of it, and they don't have time to bag and sell it themselves. They often need help keeping the stalls and pens clean. Talk to the farmer and make a deal. Chances are good that he will *pay* you to clean the stalls and give you all the manure you can tote away.

Your only investment will be for sturdy plastic bags. Get the largest size you can handle easily when full. You will also need to arrange for a way to transport the bags. If you must hire someone to haul them, it will cut into your profits. One boy made a trailer which he hitched to his bike. He hauled 12 bags at a time which he sold for $2 per bag.

Do get a state sales tax number and check on laws covering the sale of your product. If you sell door to door you may need a license.

Start out small, selling to your neighbors and family friends. Then as your reputation grows you can expand and start advertising. Read up on the advantages of all-organic fertilizers, especially your particular kind. Then you can talk intelligently with your customers.

If you don't live near a poultry, dairy, or horse farm, try to get the concession of picking up after a parade. Lots of parades have many horses and someone is required to clean up after them.

You might get paid for the work and you can sell the droppings. Use a coaster wagon and a small shovel. A child's garden set is ideal. Pull the "horse biscuits" onto the shovel with the rake or hoe. Then dump them into plastic bags. Horse droppings are usually dry and not very odiferous. The next day the bags can be flattened to break up the matter to make it easier to use. Stockyards and animal pens at fairgrounds are also potential sources.

COMPOST MERCHANT—Did you know you could turn grass clippings and dead leaves into cash? You can, by making compost out of them. Selling compost is an excellent way to earn money. There is a ready market for your product, the initial investment is small, it doesn't involve a great deal of time, and you are making a profit from a regular family chore. Since the raw materials are waste products that are usually burned or carted away, you are also helping the ecology.

Compost fertilizer is valued because it is a good way to build up soil. It also makes an excellent mulch for perennials. Mixed with soil 2 to 1, it makes one of the very best potting soils.

How to make a compost bin

1. You can use something you already have or can get at very little cost for a bin. For example, one boy uses an old bathtub. Whatever you use must drain well.

Another boy made a bin by stretching meshed wire around four corner posts. You could use 2-foot ornamental wire fencing, 4-foot chicken wire, or concrete blocks. Place your bin in a shaded area if possible, away from a building. Compost rots wood.

2. The size of your bin will depend upon the amount of clippings and leaves you have. You can start with one 4 × 4-foot bin and add to it as your business grows. If you don't have enough clippings or leaves of your own, ask neighbors for theirs.

3. To make compost, cover the floor of the bin with a 4-inch layer of clippings, weeds, leaves, and vegetable matter from kitchen waste. (No meat, or grease.) Sprinkle with water, then add another 4-inch layer of clippings. Sprinkle after each layer, unless the clippings and leaves are already moist from rain or dew.

Continue until the pile is 2 to 3 feet deep. If it is too shallow, it will dry out. If it is too deep, it is hard to turn. If your bin must be placed in the sun, cover the pile with dark plastic such as a ripped-open leaf bag.

Turn and mix your pile every two days for two weeks, bottom to top. If dry, sprinkle again. Keeping leaves moist will prevent blowing in the wind and speed up decomposition.

When the compost is black or brown and crumbly, it is ready to use. This will take 2 to 3 weeks.

If your sales are good, make another bin. Use one for ready-to-use compost and the other for fresh materials.

4. Advertise your product. You can use handbills, advertisements in the free community bulletin, or posters. If your town has a garden club, let them know about your product. Go to the library and read about the advantages of compost as a fertilizer. It will help your sales pitch to know everything you can about your product.

5. One boy has customers come to him and bring their own containers. Another bags the compost in plastic bags and delivers to his customers. Still another mixes his compost with dirt and sells potting soil.

141

TROPICAL FISH BREEDER

TONYA'S FISH FARM
Tropical Fish
Satisfaction guaranteed
Call 518-322-4605 for appointment

There's nothing fishy about the money twelve-year-old Tonya carries to the bank except the way she earns it. She has a thriving tropical fish business. Concrete blocks and 2 × 4 shelves holding 8 tanks line one wall of her bedroom and take up most of her spare time. "I have to watch them closely. A diseased fish can kill off the whole tankful in a short time," she says.

She sells to just about anyone who wants to buy, but her best customer is a pet store which has a standing order for two dozen every six weeks.

Tips on breeding tropical fish

1. This is not something to go into unless you really like fish. Make sure you have space for your tanks. Two tanks are the absolute minimum to start with. Three are better.

2. Buy a good book on breeding fish, and follow its instructions.

3. Tonya says that if you start from scratch, you probably won't make much profit trying to raise fish to sell. She already had two tanks before she started breeding her fish. "I bought a new tank each time I sold enough to pay for one, until I had eight tanks. I don't plan to expand any more," she says. "Luckily, I was able to find three good used tanks with aerators and heaters. New ones are expensive."

4. Start small, with only one or two varieties of fish. With

142

luck, under ideal conditions, 1 male and 3 females can set you up in business within six weeks.

5. Tonya recommends starting with swordtails and mollies. They are the easiest to breed and care for and they sell reasonably well.

6. Keep accurate records so you will know how much you have spent and how much you will need to charge for your fish. Food isn't expensive, but tanks, aerators, heaters, and electricity to operate them are.

7. Advertise. Tonya advertises in her free community bulletin.

8. Sell only your top-quality fish. The weak or poorly formed fish should be culled out. If you sell only top-grade merchandise, your reputation will grow and word-of-mouth advertising will sell most of your fish for you.

SMALL-ANIMAL BREEDERS—Fourteen-year-old Donald lets his rabbits do the multiplying while he adds up his profits. At present he has $500 in his savings account. He started three years ago with 2 rabbits and 2 hutches which cost him $50, paid for out of his own money. Now he has 130 rabbits and 18 hutches. Sixteen of the rabbits are his breeding stock—12 does and 4 bucks. Each year he sells around 300 rabbits, mostly for meat, but some go for pets. Meat rabbits bring him between $2.50 and $5.00. Pets bring a little more.

He estimates it costs him between $1.25 to $1.75 to raise each rabbit. His biggest expenses are for hutches or cages, feeding troughs, and watering valves. He makes enough selling by-products to feed the rabbits. Rabbit manure is one of the by-products. He sacks the manure in the empty feed sacks and sells it to garden supply stores for a ridiculously high price. It is one of the best fertilizers for roses.

Fish worms are another by-product. The worms are attracted by the rabbit droppings. Donald says he digs an average of 1000 worms per week in spring and summer from the dirt floor of the old garage where he keeps his hutches. He sells the worms to sporting goods stores for 45¢ per dozen.

Donald says, "My biggest problem has been keeping the water dishes from freezing and keeping dogs out of the garage. Dogs can do an awful lot of damage in a short time."

Raising rabbits can give you a steady income, but it is not a way to get rich quick. "Don't even start until you've read at least one good book on raising rabbits," Donald advises. "And you'd better like to keep records because you sure have a lot of records to keep."

Tips for breeders

1. Donald recommends getting 2 does and 2 bucks of good pedigreed stock directly from a breeder. Starting with 4 instead of 2 gives you a quicker return, but don't start with more. This many will net you 100 rabbits in 9 months. Build your stock from the offspring.

2. Pick your market before you pick your rabbits. Rabbits can be sold for breeding stock, meat, laboratory animals, or pets. Each market needs a different breed. Selling meat is best for beginners.

Donald sells his rabbits live to a local meat market. Others sell dressed rabbits to groceries or live rabbits to processors. One boy lines up a long list of customers to buy his rabbits and has another long list of people waiting to get on. He gets more from individuals than he can from the store, yet sells them for less than the customers would have to pay at the store.

Laboratories pay well, but usually want too many at a time for a beginner to supply. As for the pet market, rabbits produce faster than you can find customers for them.

3. Medium-sized rabbits are best for beginners because they are good for meat, eat less, reach maturity sooner, and take less space to keep than large rabbits. However, if you plan to sell to a processor, talk to him first and find out what breed he prefers.

4. Do not buy from "buy-back" concerns. You have to pay the shipping costs and this cuts your profits to almost zero.

5. All-wire hutches, either hand-made or purchased, produce the best and healthiest rabbits and are easier to clean than wood-and-wire hutches.

6. Check zoning laws in your area to be sure you are operating within the law. Donald lives in a suburban area that has no restrictions on rabbits.

7. Keep accurate records, both of breeding and of expenditures. Accurate records of breeding are a necessity to keep a good strong herd and prevent inbreeding.

HOLLIS'S HAMSTERS is the name of an eleven-year-old's firm. He got into this productive business by accident, but says he's glad it happened because he gets as much fun from it as he does profit.

"Hamsters are even better at multiplying than rabbits," he says. "If you aren't careful you will soon have a thousand good pets!"

In one year a pair of hamsters can produce 100,000 descendants. Keep that in mind before you start breeding! Think of all the cages to clean!

Another thing to think about is markets. Be sure you have a market for the offspring before you decide to go into business. Hollis had no problem selling his first litter of 8 to friends for pets, but found it much more difficult with the second and third litters which appeared about 2 and 4 months later. Before Hollis bred any more, he contacted two pet shops. Each agreed to take a dozen every 2 months at $1 each.

If you have the time and space to go into the business in a big way, hospitals, laboratories, and biological supply establishments buy large quantities. Contact them before breeding and contract for a certain number.

It costs very little to feed hamsters. Your biggest expenditures will be for cages, feeding dishes, watering bowls, and bedding materials.

Find a good book on raising hamsters and follow its instructions.

Other small animals that can be raised indoors are guinea pigs, gerbils, white rats, and white mice.

Caution—

Don't let any small rodents get loose. You could create a tremendous ecological problem because they multiply so rapidly. There is a federal law against deliberately setting them free.

146

FIREPLACE LOG BUSINESS—There are several ways to obtain raw material in this business. You can offer to cut wood on shares for someone else in the business. That is, instead of money, you are paid by getting half the wood you cut. Then you sell your half.

Or you can offer to clear a farmer's woods of dead timber. This wood usually lies until it rots, and most farmers will give you all you can pick up if you are careful not to destroy good timber.

Or you can do as three boys in Missouri did. These boys knew an opportunity when they saw it and used it to start a booming business in fireplace logs.

While riding their bikes one day, the boys passed a place where a land developer was bulldozing trees to build a sub-division. When the boys learned the trees were to be burned, they talked the man into letting them have the trees to cut into logs. The man agreed—providing the boys got the logs off the property within five days.

With the help of two friends, a bucksaw, and two axes, the boys cut the trees into logs 6 feet long, loaded them into a borrowed truck, and hauled them to one boy's home. There they cut the 6-foot lengths into 2-foot pieces. Large logs were split. Then they sold the logs, for slightly less than the going market rate, to customers who picked up their own logs. The only advertising the boys did was to place an ad like this one in the community consumer's bulletin.

FIREPLACE LOGS
Discount
if you haul them.
1246 N. Pine Street
Phone 886-3947

Sometimes farmers bulldoze scrub trees from land to reclaim it for cultivation. Often this wood is burned. When you see this being done, ask whether you can have the usable trunks for fireplace logs. The farmer might let you have the logs free. It will be hard work, but the cash return is good.

You can rent saws and axes. But if you must pay rental fees, your profit will be less. Do not rent a power saw unless you have had previous experience operating one or are supervised by an experienced adult. Power saws are dangerous.

Another possible way to get free wood is by helping to clean up tree limbs after a storm. People who do not have a fireplace must have the limbs hauled away. If you haul them, you can have them.

Caution—

Do not take any wood without permission. That is stealing and you could be prosecuted.

WATERCRESS AND MISTLETOE MERCHANTS—

Watercress—If you know a place where watercress grows, you have the perfect opportunity for making money. Watercress is a popular salad green which is expensive when bought in the grocery store. And if you live in an area where it grows wild, you can usually have all you want for the asking.

Watercress grows wild in cold, clear running water. It sometimes grows so thickly that it clogs streams. Many farmers would almost pay you to take it, just to get the stream running free again. Get permission to take the cress if it is not on your own property. Don't take anything from private property without permission.

The plants are easily pulled, so unless you have been asked to pull them to clear the stream, carefully cut the stems just

148

below the water level. Handle gently. Don't bruise the tender leaves.

Place the cress in a bucket or tub of clean ice water and keep it icy cold until sold. If you have to take the cress to the city, you will need a car. You may need an adult to help carry the tub to the car.

To sell, separate into bunches 3 or 4 inches in diameter, and tie each bunch with string or use a rubber band or paper-coated wire twister. Place your tub or bucket of cress in a coaster wagon or grocery cart and go door to door, or else take orders before gathering the cress. Check the price of cress and similar salad greens in the grocery stores, and sell yours for a little less.

If you have a large quantity, the manager of a fresh fruit and vegetable stand or grocery store might be interested in buying from you.

Mistletoe—Extra money for holiday spending can be made by selling mistletoe. Mistletoe is a parasitic plant that grows in trees in many areas. If it is not thinned occasionally, it will kill the host tree. Therefore, most people are willing to let you have all you can gather, as long as you don't damage the tree. Thirteen-year-old Freddy locates mistletoe-laden trees early in

October and tells the owners he will thin it or clear it out entirely, if that is what they want, in December.

The first week of December, Freddy passes out flyers in his neighborhood:

MISTLETOE
FRESH FROM THE TREE
50¢ large bunch
Taking orders now.
Freddy Jones
Call 736-4285

By taking orders before gathering the mistletoe, he can guarantee fresh greenery and will not end up with more than he can sell. Since most mistletoe grows high in the trees, he uses a very long pole with a device on the end for cutting the mistletoe loose. Such pruning poles can be rented by the hour from most rental service shops.

Freddy can gather about $5 worth in an hour.

10

The Recycling Business

Many enterprising teen-agers have gone into the recycling business, turning trash and discards into cash profits. The best thing about this kind of business is that almost anyone can do it and the raw materials are absolutely free. Almost anything can be recycled. What one person considers junk might be another person's treasure.

Here are some ways others have done it.

ALUMINUM RECYCLING—How would you like to help beautify the country, save energy, and earn money all at the same time? That's what 12-year-old LeeAnn does. She combines her need to earn money with her interest in ecology by collecting empty aluminum cans and selling them to a recycling company. The company pays 17¢ a pound for them.

LeeAnn pedals her bike around town looking for cans. She puts the cans in a big box in her bike basket or two heavy plastic bags which she hangs across the back fender. She finds the cans everywhere—around quick-service stores, along road-

sides, on the beach, under bleachers, in parks, and at campgrounds. She also collects cans from her neighbors.

"It's kind of funny," she says. "I never liked picking up my room, but this is different. It's like finding seventeen cents every time I get twenty-three cans." LeeAnn also keeps a large box in the trunk of the family car to hold cans found on family outings.

Her biggest problem has been storage. She usually keeps the cans until she has 100 pounds. Aluminum is light and 2,000 cans make quite a pile. LeeAnn flattens the cans and stores them in tightly sealed plastic bags beside the garage until she has enough, then her dad helps her haul them to the recycling center.

How to do it

1. Before you start this business, locate the nearest aluminum recycling center. Check your local telephone directory for the center in your area. If there isn't one in your town, write to Reynolds Aluminum Recycling Co., P.O. Box 27003, Richmond, Va. 23261, for a free directory of aluminum recycling centers. You can also call The Aluminum Association Inc.'s toll-free number 800-223-6830 to find the location of the nearest recycling center.

2. Contact the nearest center to find out when and where they accept scrap aluminum. Some companies send trucks to nearby towns and to various sections of large cities. Find out whether your nearest company does this. Also find out how much they pay per pound, the minimum number of pounds they will accept at one time, and whether they buy other types of aluminum besides cans. Some companies buy all types including pie plates, foil, frozen food and dinner trays, dip pans, pudding and meat containers, and scrap aluminum from such things as siding, rain gutters, storm doors and windows, and lawn furniture tubing (if they are cut up into 3-foot pieces).

3. To determine whether a can or other piece of metal is aluminum, buy a small magnet and test the tops and sides. If the magnet doesn't stick, it is aluminum.

4. To keep down insect and rodent pests, store your cans in plastic bags. Flatten your scrap aluminum to make it take up less space.

5. Let friends and neighbors know you are collecting aluminum. Ask them to save all their scrap aluminum for you. Promise to collect it at the same time each week or every two weeks. Then be sure to do so. Ask them to set their bags or boxes on the curb so they won't need to be disturbed.

6. You will need help to take the cans to the recycling center unless yours will accept small amounts at a time. If you have room to store a large amount, see if you can make a deal with the recycling company to pick the aluminum up when you get a truckload.

7. If you need more information, you can write The Aluminum Association Inc. for a booklet called "How to Start Your Own Aluminum Can Recycling Program." The address is 818 Connecticut Avenue N.W., Washington, D.C. 20006.

OTHER METALS—Other metals can also be recycled. Scrap iron which is junking up the countryside can be made into steel. There are scrap metal buyers in most areas who will pay for junked washers, refrigerators, lawn mowers, parts of cars, or any other pieces of iron.

Your local scrap company can help you get started. A friend who drives can make a good partner, especially if he owns a pickup truck.

Back in the thirties, people often drove through the country looking for scrap iron. Sometimes they stopped at farms and offered to buy junked farm equipment. Although this is seldom done today, it could be profitable now. You could offer to pay a fraction of what you will be getting per pound. Just be sure that you will be collecting enough scrap metal to make it worth your while. You will need to figure in the cost of gasoline.

RECYCLING OLD NEWSPAPERS—Collecting old newspapers and selling them to a wastepaper dealer is one of the ways Rick earns money. This is a pretty good way to earn money because it doesn't cost him anything and he is saving trees as well as earning money.

Here is how it works

1. Contact your nearest wastepaper dealer (look under "Wastepaper" or "Paper Companies" in the yellow pages of your telephone directory). Find out how much the dealer pays, how much paper he accepts at one time, and what kind of wastepaper he buys. Some dealers buy magazines and cardboard; others don't.

If you have more than one dealer in your area, check with all of them. Sell to the one who pays most for the kind of paper you want to sell.

Rick gets paid $1.50 per 100 pounds for his newspapers which are made into recycled paper. Some companies convert wastepaper into insulation. They pay from $1 to $2 per 100 pounds during the fall and winter months, but pay much less during the summer months.

2. Get friends and neighbors to save newspapers for you. Rick makes up advertising leaflets which he passes around to all the houses in his area. He aims to have at least 40 people saving papers for him. That way he can collect about 500 pounds per week.

This is what his leaflet says:

RICK'S NEWSPAPER
COLLECTION SERVICE
Will you please save your old newspapers for me? I will collect them
every Saturday, unless it rains. Tie
them or place them in large grocery
bags and leave them on your curb.
Or if you wish, I will sack them for
you. Call Rick if you want this
service. Phone 628-3742

About one week later, Rick follows up on this leaflet with a visit to all persons not responding. Most of the people agree to save their papers for him.

3. Grocery bags make a good way to bundle newspapers because, at least in Rick's town, a large bag holds a week's supply and weighs about 15 pounds. Weigh a few bags to get an average weight. This makes it easy to estimate the number of pounds you have collected.

4. Rick made a three-wheeler from two old bicycles to use especially for collecting his papers. It is equipped with a large wire basket in the rear. Or you can use a coaster wagon or make a trailer to hitch behind your bike.

5. Store the papers in a garage or basement to keep them dry until you have 500 pounds or more.

6. Ask an adult to help you take them to the wastepaper dealer.

EMPTY BOTTLE COLLECTING—If your state has deposit bottles, collecting and selling returnable soft-drink bottles is a good way to earn extra pocket money. You can get 5¢ to 15¢ per bottle, depending on its size and where you live. Bottles can be found along roadways, in parks and campgrounds, under bleachers, and around building sites. You can also check with your neighbors. Many people don't like to bother with returning empty bottles. They let them accumulate until the garage overflows with them. Most of these people will gladly give you half the money you collect, just for cashing the bottles in for them. If the bottles are dirty, wash them before returning them. Some places won't accept dirty bottles.

In some areas you can also cash in on non-returnable jars and bottles. Some glass companies pay 1¢ a pound for glass when it is separated according to color. It doesn't matter whether the glass is broken or not.

GOLF BALLS—A girl who lives near a golf course recycles lost golf balls. Many balls come over the fence onto her family's

property. She finds others along the road beside the golf course.

"Don't look for balls when there are a lot of golfers on the course," she warns. "You might get hit."

A boy received permission to retrieve balls from the pond at the golf course. He uses a snorkel and dives to find the balls. These two young people sell their balls at the pro shop.

GARAGE SALES—Juanita and Darla, two Cadette Girl Scouts, held a garage sale to help finance a trip to their Our Cabaña in Mexico, one of four world centers of the World Association of Girl Guides and Girl Scouts. They earned around $125 each.

Here's how they did it. Early in the spring, before cleaning time, they asked friends, neighbors, and relatives to save all their discards for them, regardless of the condition.

"We didn't turn anything down. You never know what people will buy. They will buy almost anything if the price is right," says Juanita.

When the girls thought they had enough for a sale, they set a date for a weekend when many workers in their area had a payday. Darla's garage was chosen for the sale because it was nearer to the most traffic. They placed ads in the daily newspaper and community bulletins that would come out one or two days before the sale. They also posted signs around town.

The girls sorted through everything, mended and repaired what they could, polished and shined everything that needed it, and priced each item. Felt-tipped pens were used to write the price on squares of masking tape which they stuck to each item. (Self-sticking labels you can write on are good if you have some.)

"Pricing is the hardest part and takes the most time. We set our prices realistically. We'd rather get a dime for something than have it left over," says Darla. "We are also open to bargaining."

The day before the sale, the girls set up card tables and ping-pong tables and worked hard to achieve an attractive display of their goods. Clothing was hung from a rope stretched across one end of the garage. All items of similar nature were placed together—dishes, jewelry, children's toys, books, and so forth.

On the day of the sale the girls placed signs on street corners near Darla's house and a large sign in front of the garage.

Everything not sold by Sunday at 6 P.M. was packed up. "We plan to hold another sale this fall, before it gets too cold," says Juanita. "We'll attract a different crowd looking for different things."

The girls recommend

1. Have at least $20 in small coins for change. Don't accept checks from anyone you don't know personally.

2. When setting a date, pick a weekend that comes immediately after payday if you live in a community where this is a factor. People have more money to spend then. Weekends are better than weekdays because people who work can attend.

3. The greater the variety of items you have for sale, the better your sales will be. "Don't hesitate to put something up for sale just because it doesn't work. We sold two TV sets that didn't work for ten dollars each. People buy things to rebuild or for spare parts."

4. Ping-pong tables, sawhorses with planks, and card tables make good display tables. Keep an aisle between tables so people can get around them easily.

5. Before your sale, visit other garage sales in your area to find out how similar items are being priced.

6. Save leftovers for a later sale.

7. If the weather turns bad and not many people come, just reset the date for a couple of weeks later. You've already done most of the work.

8. "We divide our profits equally so we don't have to keep track of who brought what," says Darla.

9. Sample ad for newspaper:

SUPER BIG GARAGE SALE
4162 N. Walnut.
Friday and Saturday, June 29–30.
Hundreds of items priced to sell—
clothing, books, toys, appliances,
sporting goods, TV, and plenty of
other goodies.

10. Be sure to check local regulations concerning garage sales. In some areas a license or permit is necessary. There may also be rules governing the number of days and hours a sale may be held or the number of sales you may hold in any one calendar year.

11

Make Your Hobby Pay

With a little know-how, most hobbies can be turned into moneymakers. Yours might not make you rich, but it can earn you some pocket money or at least pay for itself.

Here are some ways it has been done.

TAPE RECORDING—Two sophomore boys have turned their hobby into a very profitable business and had fun doing it. They make tapes of weddings, award dinners, confirmations, christenings, graduation exercises, and recitals which they sell to persons wanting lasting mementos of important days in their lives. Brides are the boys' most frequent customers, but the boys also sell tapes to parents, grandparents, and sometimes teen-agers.

The boys saved from their allowances to help pay for their equipment and borrowed the remainder from their fathers, whom they were able to pay back within a few weeks from their earnings.

To find customers, the boys read the society pages of the daily newspaper. Then they contact individuals or organiza-

tions personally and explain their services and fees. They don't advertise because they are busy every spare minute of their free time without doing so.

To go into this kind of business, you need to know a great deal about recording equipment and tapes. These boys had been recording as a hobby for more than a year before they went into business and were quite proficient at it. Although their equipment was expensive, their end product sold well and at a high rate of profit.

Important tips

1. Buy the very best equipment you can afford.

2. Contact potential customers well in advance of the event. Get a written agreement that they will pay on delivery.

3. Give your company a catchy name and a snappy slogan. Print cards with the company name and telephone number and your name and address to give to all potential customers.

4. Arrive at the function early. Locate the best place to set up your equipment and have it in place before guests arrive. Make sure that all concerned are notified that you will be taping the proceedings.

5. Be sure your equipment is in top working order. Don't let weak batteries spoil a sale or disappoint a customer. Buy the right length tape. Thirty minutes is long enough for most wedding ceremonies, but not for a concert or play.

6. Be unintrusive. Don't disrupt a program or ceremony.

7. Keep accurate records of your expenses to avoid spending more than you earn. To set a reasonable fee for your service, you must know how much it costs. If you don't have competition, ask as much as you think the market will bear. A bride will probably pay more for a recording of her wedding than a parent will pay for a recording of a piano recital.

8. For other potential customers, watch for parents who take pictures of their children at school functions. Some parents will buy recordings of anything their children participate in—for example, school concerts, school plays, and vocal, instrumental, or speech contests, especially if the children are winners. Your taping could be done on speculation.

Tapes can be erased and reused if not bought. Tapes can also be duplicated and offered for sale to each member of a school program or other function.

CANDID CAMERA—Sixteen-year-old Tina's hobby is photography. It is a costly hobby, but for Tina it more than pays for itself. Although having her photos published in her local newspaper has led to free-lance assignments, she has the most fun and makes the most money snapping candid shots.

Most of her customers are schoolmates, but she also sells to parents of small children. Parents will buy almost any good picture of their kids.

From experience, Tina has learned that the kind of shots people are most apt to buy are shots that are flattering or that record momentous moments in their lives. She once earned $50 for one roll of film taken at a wedding.

Where Tina goes, her camera goes. For such things as parades, recitals, and school functions—graduation, concerts, plays and the like—she usually has several people lined up in advance who want good candid shots of the event. That way she knows whom to focus on. Then she gets the names of as many other persons in the picture that she can and offers them copies of the pictures, too.

Tina especially likes to take pictures at sports events. "The winning basket will sell, no matter which team made it," she says. "Track events are really great because there are so many contestants. Little League games are good, too. Most parents don't think to bring their cameras to the games. Sometimes the parents make better subjects than the kids."

To take candid shots, you need to know a lot about photography and cameras. Tina has studied photography for four years and has won many awards. She is the official photographer for her school yearbook.

She recommends that you use the very best camera you can afford. An automatic camera with telephoto lens is best. "You don't have time to mess around with light meters when you are taking candid shots," she says.

Important tips

1. Keep an accurate record of all expenses. It is easy to overspend. Price each picture high enough that it will pay for other pictures that don't turn out well or don't sell.

2. According to Tina, colored pictures sell best. It is cheaper to have colored film developed than to do it yourself.

3. Carry a notebook and pencil to jot down names and addresses of as many persons in your shot as possible. Unless you know the people personally, give them a card with your name and telephone number. Tell them you will call as soon as the film is developed. Then do so and make an appointment to show the shots.

4. Take more than one shot of the same scene whenever possible. One may not turn out well.

5. Go to all functions early so that you can get a good seat up front.

6. Try not to disturb others with your picture taking. Keep it unobtrusive.

7. Never flash flashbulbs in people's faces.

8. Never take unflattering pictures or people in embarrassing situations. They won't sell and it will hurt your reputation as a sensitive photographer.

9. Another way to make money from photography is by taking candid camera shots on the street with a Polaroid camera, especially in tourist areas. Tourists seldom get pictures of themselves while visiting interesting places. Most people buy good shots of themselves having a good time.

Snapping candid shots of dinner parties at a local restaurant can also be profitable, but ask the owner or manager of the restaurant for permission first.

This is the ad one boy places in the community shoppers' guide to advertise his services:

YOUR FRIENDLY NEIGHBORHOOD PHOTOGRAPHER
HAVE CAMERA, WILL TRAVEL
Birthday parties my specialty.
Alex Smith   536-4279

166

PRINTING—

SMALL JOBS PRESS
PERSONALIZING OUR SPECIALTY
Brian Libran   Call 339-4687
For rates

Printer's ink is in fourteen-year-old Brian's blood. The time came when he had printed more than enough on his small hand press of everything that his family could use or give as gifts. Then he decided to cash in on his friends' requests that he do printing jobs for them and began printing things for others for a small fee. Now he has all the printing jobs he wants and earns enough to buy bigger and better equipment plus having a little extra cash to spend on other things.

Besides personalizing stationery, party napkins, and greeting cards, Brian prints personalized recipe cards, bookplates, and business cards for friends. He also prints receipts and invoices for fellow classmates who have gone into business for themselves.

To go into this kind of business you need to own a press and be a dedicated printer. Hand typesetting is slow work, but if you enjoy printing, you might as well earn money doing it. Your overhead is low. You can get a small hand press, which is adequate for beginning, and all other necessary equipment for less than photographic or tape-recording equipment costs.

Important tips
1. Buy and read a good book on printing as a hobby.

2. Start small. Do single-line jobs such as personalizing party napkins and stationery until you have gained experience; then expand.

3. Have your customers supply their own stationery, napkins, or whatever. Advise them that you will need at least a dozen extra to allow for proofing and goofs.

4. Set your fee for a job before you start setting type. From experience you should know how long it will take you to complete a given job. Charge accordingly.

5. Set a date when the job should be finished. Then deliver on time.

6. Don't overextend yourself. Keep accurate records of job orders so you won't get them mixed up. A logbook will help you organize your time and prevent your taking more orders for one week than you can possibly finish.

7. Give your press a snappy name (something original) and print up a business card to hand to potential customers. This should include your name, telephone number, and rates (by the word or line). It will also prevent people from asking you to do work as a favor.

8. Word of mouth will be your best advertising. Most of your potential customers will probably have seen samples of your work.

9. As long as you are selling services only, or are being paid for just labor, you will not need a tax number. You probably will not need a license to operate, but do check your community regulations to be sure.

HAND-TYING FISH FLIES—Thirteen-year-old Jeremy was an avid fisherman before an accident put him in a wheelchair for several months. When his father gave him a fly-tying kit to occupy his time, Jeremy never dreamed it would turn into a thriving business.

Fascinated by the hobby, Jeremy's creative mind and nimble fingers fashioned hundreds of beautiful flies. He could hardly wait until he was able to try them out.

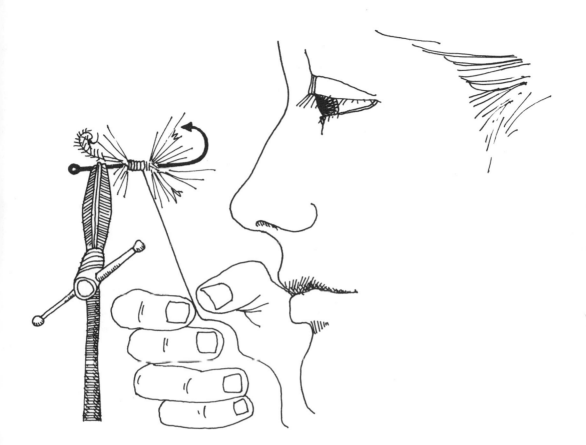

The flies proved so successful that other fishermen wanted to know what Jeremy used for bait. Upon seeing his beautiful flies, just about everyone wanted one. Jeremy began making flies to sell. Now almost every fisherman in his area has at least one "Jeremy Fly."

Jeremy maintains that the secret to successful fly tying is in knowing what kind of fish will bite on each type of fly. "What will catch one kind of fish is no good for another," he says.

The demand for his flies soon outgrew his small fly kit so Jeremy invested in more materials, which can be purchased in any hobby shop. Jeremy uses fur, silk, wool, tinsel, and feathers. According to him, yellow and brown feathers are the best.

Although Jeremy has done quite well at selling his flies to individuals, a fourteen-year-old girl made a small fortune selling her special trout fly through dealers all over the country. She has sold more than 100,000 of them.

Tips for fly-tying business

1. To be a successful fly tier, you need to be an avid fisherman and know your fish as well as your flies.

2. There are several good books on the market or in your library on tackle making. Read the sections on fly tying.

3. It is best to start with a small hobby kit which can be obtained from most hobby shops for a few dollars. Jeremy spent hours tying flies and many more hours trying them out before he discovered winning combinations.

4. You can sell flies outright to shops and fishermen, or you can try to get bait shops to sell your flies on commission.

5. If you have developed a really good fly, you can advertise it in sports magazines. Jeremy plans to place this advertisement in two of the leading sports magazines next season.

"JEREMY FLIES"
Tested and proven successful
by hundreds of fishermen.
Write for price list
P.O. Box 446, Clarksvale, Mo. 65003

DOLL HOSPITAL—

ST. JAMES DOLL HOSPITAL
Free Estimates
Emergency service
Call Clara   456-8321

Fifteen-year-old Clara has been collecting dolls for three years. "Many of them are in pretty sad shape when I get them," she says, "because I don't have much money to spend. I had to learn how to mend them myself."

She makes new bodies from cloth and sometimes combines parts from two or more dolls. Occasionally she buys a head, wig, or arms and legs for a rare doll. Clara's workshop is in the family garage and the neighborhood children often gather to watch her work. Of course they bring their own broken dolls to Clara to be mended.

When Clara realized that she was mending as many dolls for others as for herself, she decided to open a doll hospital. She calls it St. James Hospital because St. James is her last name. "It sounds kind of important. Little girls like to say their dolls are at St. James Hospital."

Clara advertises by putting posters in laundromats and grocery stores. She also places ads in the free community bulletin and in a doll collectors' newsletter. Some of her customers are other doll collectors, but many are little girls whose dolls have lost an arm or leg. "I try to replace the missing limbs with used parts because they look more like the rest of the doll, but if I can't I order a part." Clara buys spare parts from a wholesaler, but hairpins, paper clips, and rubber bands take care of the most common problems.

Clara doesn't keep a large inventory of parts, because there are too many different kinds of dolls. She receives most ordered pieces in just a few days. The price she charges for mending a doll is based on the amount of time and work involved and on the new parts needed. Collectors' dolls usually take more work than a little girl's doll.

Clara's tips
1. Keep a careful inventory of all parts on hand. It won't do you much good to have a part if you don't know you have it.
2. Keep good records of all money spent and time used to make repairs.
3. Buy old and broken dolls wherever possible—they can

172

be found at garage sales and thrift shops. Also ask customers to bring in unwanted dolls. These often can be used for spare parts.

4. Give free estimates if possible before beginning work. Sometimes the repair will cost more than the doll is worth.

5. Buy a good book on doll collecting and doll repair. You can't survive without it.

Clara says, "Half the fun of having a doll hospital is the joy in the face of a little girl when she picks up her mended doll."

BIRD BREEDER—Although fourteen-year-old Ronnie raises finches, his is not a fly-by-night venture. What started out as a hobby has turned into a flourishing business for this enterprising young man.

Ronnie began with 4 finches, two males and two hens, which he had bought for pets. To make them comfortable he screened a small, little-used patio area, added two potted trees and several large planters filled with house plants, and let the birds fly freely throughout the area. He left the floor bare to make it easier to hose down daily, and he placed nesting boxes and nesting materials where the birds could find them. Then he waited.

The birds were so happy in their new home that within a short time they began nesting and laying eggs. In three weeks Ronnie's flock had tripled. By the end of the summer he had over 100 birds, many more than could comfortably live in the screened area, so he began selling the young birds to friends. He sold them two or three at a time because finches like company.

But his birds were so prolific that it was obvious Ronnie would either need to reduce his breeding stock or find another outlet for their offspring. He contacted a local pet shop and after he received a city health inspection and a license, the shop agreed to take all the birds he could provide. Ronnie also advertises in the local newspaper and sells to individuals who prefer to buy from a breeder. He estimates it costs him about $2 per bird to raise. He gets from $10 to $15 per pair. In one year he sold 250 birds. He lives in southern California so the birds breed year round.

Tips for bird breeders

1. It is best to buy your breeding stock from a breeder rather than from a pet store. The birds will be healthier and stronger for not having been shipped. You can also ask the breeder what kind of food they are used to.

2. Finches are best to start with because they take a minimum amount of care, cost less than canaries, and are subject to fewer diseases.

3. The cage should be large and airy, with plenty of access to light but not boiling sun. Outdoor cages should be frost-free and dustproof, away from drafts.

4. Be sure you have a market for your birds before you breed very many.

5. If you sell yours at a competitive price you should have no problem selling them.

6. Check local laws to be sure you are operating within the law, especially if you have outdoor cages.

7. Several good books on bird care are on the market. It is advisable to buy one to keep as a handy reference.

Some young people raise game fowl which they sell to sporting clubs. Others raise racing pigeons.

HOUSE PLANT SALES—Are you a house plant lover? Fourteen-year-old Alice's hobby is starting new plants from old. But her mother complained when the house overflowed with plants. Here's how Alice keeps her hobby under control and makes money doing it. She has a plant sale in her garage twice a year—once in spring and once in fall. She averages $50 per sale, so now her mother lets her start all the new plants she wants and doesn't complain.

How to make money from house plants

Almost everyone has a plant or two. Many people would enjoy more if they could buy healthy, hardy plants at reasonable prices. This is a need you can fill if you are already a plant hobbyist.

Most plants need to be trimmed or cut back frequently to be kept healthy and beautiful. Alice saves all the trimmings from her coleus, philodendron, devil's ivy, wandering Jew, geraniums, and other plants. She roots them in water-filled jars. She also starts new plants from runners of cymbidium, spider plants, and strawberry saxifrage, and the leaves of African violets. Runner plants are potted in half-pint milk cartons from Alice's school cafeteria, or in bleach jugs. African violets are potted in recycled Styrofoam cups.

Using recycled items for pots enables Alice to keep her overhead low. Therefore, she can price her plants low enough to sell well. However, the large variety and hardiness of her plants helps sales as much as the low cost. "People like to have a lot to choose from," she says. That's why she begs cuttings from any plant she does not have.

At her first sale Alice sold only rooted cuttings in water. Thus she had no overhead. With her profits she bought potting soil, plastic bags, and vermiculite and added potted plants and vermiculite-rooted cuttings at her next sale. The vermiculite-rooted cuttings proved to be one of her best-selling items.

Three or four weeks before a sale, Alice pours 2 to 3 inches of vermiculite into the bottom of several plastic bags. Then she inserts one or two cuttings as deeply as they'll go into the vermiculite in each bag, and adds water. The bag is pulled up snugly around the stems and closed with a twister. Then Alice folds the top over, above the cuttings, and fastens with a paper clip. Customers like these because they are easier to transport without being damaged. The customers can see the roots, too. The roots should be at least 2 inches long and ready for potting.

You could save on overhead by recycling the plastic bags such as those used as "raincoats" for your home-delivered newspaper. Bread wrappers could be used, but would need more vermiculite because of their size.

Alice suggests that on the day of the sale you arrange your plants as attractively as possible on card tables. She says you should have at least 50 plants with 5 to 10 varieties from which to choose. It takes Alice six months to get enough for a sale. Alice occasionally adds sweet-potato vines, pineapple plants, avocado, grapefruit, and lemon trees to her offerings. These plants cost nothing to start and only the soil to pot. They will need to be started at least 6 months before your planned sale, however.

For the first sale, Alice placed an ad in the free community bulletin. Now she places the ad and a sign in her yard announcing the time and date of her sale. However, word of mouth is her best advertisement. Her best customers are regulars, who frequently inquire when her next sale will be.

Tips to remember
1. Keep your overhead low so that your price will be competitive.

2. Make sure all plants offered for sale are hardy and healthy.

176

3. Make your display as attractive as possible.
4. Start out small. Use first profits to expand.
5. Work toward as large a variety as space and time allow.
6. Build your reputation and use it to attract more business.
7. Unusual plants sell better than common ones.
8. Keep accurate records of costs and price accordingly.

12

Cash from Your Kitchen

If you like to cook, you have a salable skill. Almost everyone who enjoys cooking has some particular food that they cook better than anything else. That food is their specialty. Many young people have earned money selling their specialties to people who don't like to cook.

Here are some success stories.

OVEN SPECIALTIES—Most people like home-baked goodies better than those bought in stores. Some people can't eat foods with artificial additives and can't eat commercially baked goods. Others either can't or don't have time to bake. This creates a big demand for home-baked goodies. And that's how you can earn money—by meeting this demand. Many youth groups earn money by holding bake sales in shopping centers. Each member donates one or two items which are priced and set out on card tables. Cakes, cookies, pies, breads, brownies, and cupcakes sell very well.

Fifteen-year-old Anita was surprised when the four loaves

179

of bread she baked for her youth group bake sale sold quickly at $1.25 per loaf. When she heard one satisfied customer say, "If I could find someone who baked bread like this in my neighborhood, I'd buy a couple of loaves every week," Anita went into business. She signed the lady up for two loaves of bread weekly and asked her to tell others that she would bake bread for them, too. She now has six regular customers who buy two loaves per week, and several others who special-order loaves on occasion.

Anita relies upon word of mouth for most of her advertising. Occasionally she bakes miniature loaves for gifts. These always bring in new customers, but six is about all she can handle through the school year.

"I like baking bread," says Anita. "I get rid of a lot of tension slapping, pounding, and kneading the dough."

When ten-year-old Ramon needed money to help pay for a new bike, he turned to his favorite hobby—baking. Using cake mix and cupcake liners, he made and sold cupcakes door to door and in six weeks he had enough money to buy his bike.

Louise has been baking cookies every Saturday for more than a year. That was no problem as long as her brothers were home to eat them all. But when they left home the deep freeze overflowed because Louise still baked. Her solution was to sell the excess cookies.

She went door to door offering free samples and taking orders, selling cookies by the dozen. This worked very well for her. Now she bakes every Saturday and earns money doing it.

Thirteen-year-old Coralee's specialty is blueberry muffins. The demand for them is almost more than she can keep up with. Coralee's customers call in their orders and she bakes each morning she has an order to fill.

Suzi makes pies which she sells to a café that advertises "homemade pies." She is most famous for her coconut cream and lemon meringue pies. "Apple pies are too expensive because it takes so much time to make them," she says.

HEALTH FOODS
Custom Baked—Made by Order
WHEAT GERM HONEY BREAD
$1.50 per 1 lb. loaf
Call 632-6548
Delivered day after tomorrow

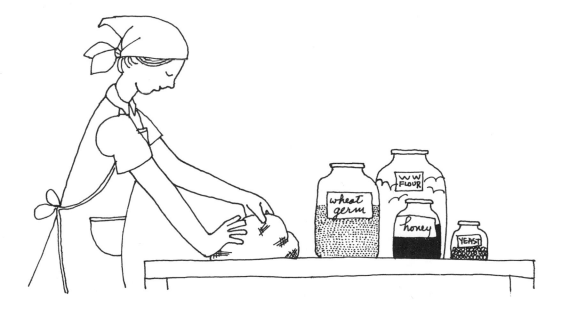

Fifteen-year-old Mary Jane combines her high school cooking class skills with the popularity of health foods to earn money. Her specialty is wheat germ honey bread. She baked a loaf which her mother served at a brunch. It was so delicious that many guests wanted the recipe. Mary Jane suggested that she bake the bread for them and got six orders on the spot. She now has a long list of regular customers. Her only request is that she receive all orders at least three days before the delivery date. Since her bread is best if left to set overnight, this gives her plenty of advance notice and makes it easier to adjust her schedule to meet the demand.

Mary Jane also has a standing order from a local health food store for 10 loaves each week. She gives the store a discount for buying in quantity. Mary Jane keeps careful records of her costs. Her price per loaf is based on the cost of the ingredients and of the plastic wrappers and oven heat. She charges extra to deliver.

Other types of health food such as wheat germ cookies and carrot bread or cake can be baked and sold from your kitchen.

Tips for home bakers

1. Keep exact records of all expenses including gasoline if you deliver. Don't forget to add the cost of electricity or gas for baking.

2. Start small. Don't buy a lot of ingredients until you are sure your specialty will catch on. Then use your profits to invest in large quantities of ingredients. Large sizes cost less per unit than small sizes.

3. Buy only top-grade ingredients. Quality pays in the long run.

4. Make absolutely sure that you and your kitchen are spotlessly clean.

182

5. Check local laws to be sure you are operating within the law. In some areas food handlers must pass health examinations.

6. Word-of-mouth advertising is best but is limited. Mary Jane places posters in laundromats and other places around town, and advertises in the free weekly community paper.

7. Line up regular customers who will buy one or more orders every week. Then you will have a weekly income you can count on. Don't turn down special orders. They often lead to regular ones.

8. Be dependable. Always deliver on time.

CAKE DECORATING—Sixteen-year-old Teresa is a talented cake decorator. She has been baking and decorating cakes by special order ever since her decorated cake won first place at the county fair. A cake-decorating class at the YWCA started Teresa on her career. Most of her cakes are sheet cakes for children's birthday parties.

"Some of them are real challenges. People want all kinds of things from cakes shaped like a football to Donald Duck," she says. Teresa takes pictures of each cake to show to customers. "But I'll try anything they want. I charge more if I've never made one like it before, because it takes more time to create a new design."

Teresa also takes cake orders for showers. "I've never been asked to do a wedding cake. I don't think I'm quite ready for that yet," she says.

She uses a simple cake mix to make the cakes. "Because," she says, "I'm really much better at decorating than baking. Kids are more interested in how a cake looks than how it tastes. Sometimes customers bake their own cakes and bring them to me to decorate."

CAKE DECORATING
Done in my home.
Specializing in birthday cakes
Call 333-4007

This is the ad Teresa places in her community's free shoppers' guide. If you are a skilled cake decorator, you might consider decorating cookies as well as cakes. There is usually a good market for both birthday cakes and holiday cookies. Select a list of likely customers in your neighborhood and give them a hand-printed or typed announcement of your services.

CANDY COMPANY—Everyone raved about the pralines Jody and Lisa made for a party at their father's office. So the girls put their heads together and came up with a winning moneymaking idea. They thought that if everyone liked them so well, maybe they would buy some. To test their idea, they made four dozen pralines. They bagged each praline separately in a plastic bag and packed the lot in a large box along with a jar that had a slot in the lid. To the box they taped this hand-printed sign:

JODY & LISA'S PRALINES
15¢ each   2 for 25¢
Drop money here.

They asked their father to take the pralines to work and place them on a table near office traffic. The box was empty before noon! The girls were in business.

The next week they sent 6 dozen and again sold out. They continue to send 6 dozen to the office every week, and also

Judy & Lisa's Pralines 15¢ each 2 for 25¢ DROP MONEY HERE

contacted the manager of a gift shop who agreed to sell the pralines on commission. The manager provides empty boxes for the girls which they pack with pralines.

How you can do it

1. Pralines are so well liked they sell anywhere, any time, even though they are relatively expensive. If you are good at making candy, you might want to try your luck with these.

2. Keep accurate records of all costs. Pralines do not have many ingredients, but those they do have are expensive. Your only other overhead will be plastic bags. Don't forget to add to your costs record any materials you use to promote your product.

3. To save on overhead, Jody and Lisa buy whole pecans which they crack and shell themselves. "We'd pick them, too, if we could," they said.

If you live in a pecan-growing area, consider picking the nuts on shares to cut down on overhead.

4. Before trying to sell pralines at an office, check whether this would be permissible. Some places will not allow it.

5. You can also sell pralines at ball games. Stand near the ticket office with a bright box full of pralines. You can hang the box from your neck with a ribbon to free your hands. If your price is posted in plain sight, you will increase your sales. Make sure you have plenty of small coins on hand to make change.

6. If there are no laws in your city prohibiting it, stand on the sidewalk in front of a large office building or a shopping center, or anyplace where large numbers of people circulate.

7. If you live in an area where peanuts are more plentiful than pecans, peanut brittle might make a better business venture for you. If you live in Hawaii, try macadamia nut brittle.

Fourteen-year-old Matthew earns his Christmas money making peanut brittle which is a favorite holiday goody in his area. His mother and dad take samples to work and bring back orders for him to fill.

"I like filling orders better than making candy on speculation," he says. "Knowing I'll get paid for all I make gives me more incentive."

JELLIES AND JAMS—Justin, 13, and his sister, Lea, make and sell jelly to earn spending money. These venturesome

youngsters only need buy sugar and pectin for their product because they pick their fruit free along country roads. They ride their bikes to the country to locate fruit which they pick and put into one-gallon buckets. The buckets are equipped with lids to prevent spillage on the way home.

They wash, stem, and cook the fruit; then they pour off the juice and make it into jelly. The jelly is poured into baby food and small mayonnaise jars and a hand-stamped label is fastened to each jar.

HOMEMADE JELLY
No additives
WILD GRAPE
Ingredients–wild grape juice, sugar, & pectin

The children also make jelly from blackberries, wild plums, and elderberries. They make jam from blackberries, dewberries, and gooseberries.

Justin figures the cost of the sugar and pectin, and takes into consideration the amount of time to pick the fruit and to make the jelly when setting the price for each jar.

Homemade jelly sells well—especially wild grape and elder-berry, which usually cannot be found in stores. Beach plum jelly is popular in New England. A good selling point for home-made jelly is that it has no additives. Justin points this out in his advertising.

He hand-prints leaflets which he leaves door to door. On the leaflets he lists the flavors and their prices along with his name and telephone number. Once a year Justin and his sister hold a special sale in their garage. This sale is advertised in the local newspaper and by posters around town.

Justin comments, "It is a lot of work, but how else could we earn that much money?"

How to do it

1. If you know where you can pick a lot of wild fruit free, pick it and help your mother or father make it into jelly. When you have made all your family can use, pick more fruit and then make and sell the jelly.

2. Ask permission before picking wild fruit on private property. If you do not damage other things on the land and do not forget to close gates, usually you will be given permission to pick on private land. Much of the fruit goes to waste because no one picks it.

3. If you don't have access to wild fruit, pick fruit on shares and convert your damaged, bruised, or overripe fruit into jelly.

4. Put the jelly in recycled glass containers to cut down on overhead. If you don't have a baby in your family, ask friends or neighbors who do to save their empty baby food jars for you.

5. Keep accurate records. You need to know the exact cost of each jar of jelly in order to price it.

CATERING—Sixteen-year-old Shannon is a sandwich maker. She loves the challenge of creating unique tasty sandwiches to fit every occasion. Folks in her home town call Shannon to order her famous bite-sized party sandwiches for afternoon parties, or her giant jumbo sandwiches for teen-age bashes, or just plain taste treats for picnics. Most of her orders are for one of her specialties, but sometimes clients ask for something new and original. In a busy week she can earn a lot of money.

How to go into this business

Shannon recommends that you volunteer your services to a few organizations to establish your reputation. "Be creative in design and taste combinations. Taste-test everything. Eye appeal is important, but taste is more important," she says. Then let it be known that you are available to cater sandwiches for individuals. Word of mouth will be all the advertising you will need if you do as well as she does.

1. Keep accurate accounts of all costs. Your price per dozen sandwiches must be based on the cost of ingredients plus the time required to make them. Charge extra if you must deliver.

2. You can cut down on overhead by buying precooked boneless ham and having it sliced into sandwich thickness. It is much cheaper than packaged ham slices.

3. Ask clients to phone orders at least a week in advance. That will give you plenty of time to assemble all ingredients.

4. It is best to stick with a few basic sandwich types until you are well established. Make it a point to find out which kinds of sandwiches are most popular with each age group in your area. Work on these. Improve upon them. Be original in shapes and sizes.

5. Shannon cuts her time in half by making sandwiches assembly-line method.

6. She places open-faced party sandwiches on Styrofoam meat trays and covers them with plastic wrap. Other types are individually wrapped in plastic sandwich bags.

7. Make sandwiches the same day as delivery date, unless they must be delivered very early or your order is for more than you can possibly make up in one time. Fresh sandwiches mean more sales. Keep them refrigerated until delivered.

8. If you know a business that has many employees but no cafeteria, consider making sandwiches to sell to workers during their lunch break. Consider the type of worker and construct your sandwiches accordingly.

9. You can also cater canapés, party cookies, pizzas, or any other food item popular in your area.

GROUP EFFORTS—

Pancake sales

You've heard the expression "sold like hotcakes." A troop of Cadette Scouts found that anything that sells like hotcakes does very well indeed. They were looking for a way to earn money to help finance a trip to Washington, D.C., one summer, and decided that if hotcakes sell so well they should give them a try.

How they did it

The twelve girls set up committees. The finance committee figured the cost of supplies and how much they would need to charge, based on an estimate of 150 customers. The supplies included ingredients for the hotcakes, napkins, paper plates and cups, butter, brown sugar and maple flavoring for syrup, plastic forks and spoons, coffee and canned orange juice.

One committee was responsible for finding a suitable location and date. They decided upon a shopping center parking lot located across the street from a large office building. They received permission to move under the awnings in case of rain. They decided upon a Friday for the date because it was one of the busiest shopping days as well as a working day. The merchants at the shopping center agreed to donate the electricity since the girls were a part of a non-profit organization.

Another committee was in charge of collecting all necessary equipment including picnic tables and benches for serving, four electric griddles, and two large coffee urns.

The fourth committee was in charge of advertising. They made posters and placed them in windows all around town a week before the sale. They also arranged for spot announcements on the local radio station and an ad in the free community bulletin.

190

The day before the sale, half the girls built the booth from scrap lumber. The other half mixed enough ingredients to make 700 hotcakes. The mix was then stored in empty coffee cans to be mixed with water as needed just before cooking.

The girls also made their own syrup from brown sugar, water, and maple flavoring, which was bottled in quart jars and served in small cream pitchers.

Although their posters stated "all you can eat," few took more than four. "It was a lot of work and took lots of organizing, but it was worth it," the girls said.

Fish fry

A church youth group earned money by holding a fish fry. They bought frozen fish steaks which they deep-fried in electric ovens, and served with coleslaw and coffee. They had an advantage in that they could serve from their church recreation hall.

Chili supper

Another youth group had a chili supper. The chili was prepared at home and kept hot in electric roasters. They measured. the exact number of bowlfuls each roaster would hold. They also served coleslaw and coffee with the chili. The cabbage was sliced ahead of time, mixed with dressing, and kept fresh in ice chests.

Tips to consider

1. These are good moneymaking ideas for groups, but remember that "organization" is the key word for a venture of this kind. All costs must be figured before you lay out any cash. You could lose money rather than make it if everything is not carefully planned down to the last detail.

2. Keep accurate records of each transaction.

3. Get as much equipment and supplies donated as possible. Buy supplies in quantity and take advantage of store discounts given to organizations.

4. Churches, YMCA or YWCA, and empty store buildings are possible places for holding your sales. Estimate your profit based on the number of units you figure you can sell; then decide whether you can afford the rent.

5. Check with local authorities to make sure you are operating within the law.

6. For greatest success, choose a food item that is popular in your area, is fairly inexpensive to make, simple to prepare, and can be prepared at least partly ahead of time.

7. At least one person should be an expert at cooking the food chosen. If not, then find someone who is, to supervise.

8. Advertise with hand-printed posters placed around the neighborhood and in front of the building you are using.

OTHER WAYS TO EARN CASH FROM YOUR KITCHEN—Are you good at baking pies? Four high school girls made a pile of money at a boat race by operating a refreshment stand from the back of a station wagon. The lake where the races were held offered no other refreshment facilities. The girls' families frequently attended the races and the girls knew from experience that people often got hungry and thirsty while watching.

The girls served lemonade, iced tea, and pies. Since they had no competition, they could charge as much as they wanted. This idea could be used anywhere there are large crowds gathered for several hours with no refreshment stands.

If you try this, be sure to keep careful records of costs. Frozen pies could be bought, if on sale. If you don't have refrigeration do not serve cream pies. They spoil too easily. Use ice chests to hold ice for tea and lemonade. Be sure to have a large container of fresh water. Frozen lemonade mix can be mixed at the site, and tea diluted there also. You will need a 50 percent markup over expenses to make this project worth your while.

Twelve-year-old Amy is a girl with a good memory. It had been very cold the day of the Christmas parade the year before, so she had taken a thermos of hot chocolate to help her keep warm while waiting for the parade to begin. People standing nearby commented that they wished they had thought of that.

So the next year Amy took a 3-gallon thermos jug of hot chocolate and 60 plastic cups. She sold hot chocolate to people standing nearby for 15¢ a cup, making $7 in profit.

13

Cash in on Your Talent

Another source of extra income is your talent. Almost everyone has a talent of some kind. For some it is one of the fine arts— music, art, dancing, writing, and that sort of thing. For others it is mechanics, typing, or just a gift of gab.

You don't need to be a child prodigy or a genius to cash in on your talent. Of course it helps and makes it easier if you are, but it isn't necessary. If you have developed and exercised your talent so that you are reasonably proficient, you can use it to earn money.

The only thing you need besides your talent is self-confidence, and that comes with practice. Some young people enter contests just for the money awards. That is self-confidence! But if you try that, make sure you don't spend more on entry fees than you could possibly win.

Many young people have put their talents to work to help earn pocket money. Some have earned enough to finance their way through college.

MUSICAL TALENT—Can you sing or play a musical instru-

ment? Cash in on it. Not everyone is as talented or as lucky as one gifted 12-year-old drummer who plays with a professional band. Her father and grandfather are professional musicians, which gives her a special edge over other talented young people. But many other talented young people without this advantage have made their musical talents pay.

Singing

Sixteen-year-old Betty often played the guitar and sang at weddings and parties for friends and relatives. As her reputation grew, she began to get requests from friends of friends. When friends of friends of friends began requesting her to sing for them, she began charging a fee for her services.

Two sisters, aged 15 and 17, specialize in singing duets for weddings and funerals. They printed cards giving their names, fees, and telephone number, and left them at all churches and funeral homes. They say they earn more money this way than they could doing anything else. It only takes a few hours of their time and does not interfere with their schooling or social life.

Others earn cash by singing with small rock groups or combos.

Piano, Organ, and Instrumental

Fifteen-year-old Maria is a talented pianist and organist. She plays the organ at a church other than her own. Many small churches do not have a trained organist or pianist in their congregation and will gladly pay a capable young player.

If you play well, write up fact sheets telling about your training and requesting an audition. Then leave one at the office of each small church in your community. Be sure to include your name and telephone number on your fact sheet. You may get

197

more offers than you can accept. You can also specialize in playing the organ or piano for weddings and funerals.

Sixteen-year-old Joan says, "I've accompanied singing classes at school since I was ten. When I was fourteen I played for so many weddings and funerals for friends and relatives that the ministers and funeral directors began recommending me to total strangers."

Many talented young musicians earn money playing other instruments—drums, flutes, violins—for civic organizations. Their first performances are usually free, but they soon have enough calls to start charging a modest fee.

Almost any town of more than 1,000 population can boast of an amateur band that can be hired to play at dances. If your town doesn't have a band and you play an instrument, look around for four or five others to join you and form a combo. If your town already has one or two combos, specialize. Specialize in something different to cut down on the competition. There are plenty of choices: sacred music, classical, country and western, pop, and hard rock. If you can't be better than your competition, then be different.

It is not necessary to want to make a career of music to make money from it. Charge only a token fee at first. Then when your reputation is well established, you can charge more.

ARTISTIC TALENT—If you are handy with a pencil, pen, or brush, this ability can be put to use to earn pocket money. You don't need to be a child prodigy like the 13-year-old whose pictures sell for hundreds of dollars and hang in museums.

Signs
Susan earned her own spending money all through high school and college by lettering signs. She prepared a sample

of her beautiful lettering and showed it to the managers of fast-food stores, small groceries, and bakeries. Then she offered to print signs for them at a price they found hard to refuse. She soon had all the work she could handle. Some of the signs they wanted were painted on poster board and were done at home. Others were painted directly on the windows.

Christmas scenes

Carmen and Rosa use their artistic talents to earn Christmas money. They paint Christmas scenes on store and office windows with poster paint. They begin around Thanksgiving by painting scenes on the front doors of their school and on the large plate-glass windows of their public library without charge.

They take colored photographs of these scenes along with hand-printed business cards and sample sketches to discount stores, insurance offices, realtors, law offices, bakeries, automobile agencies, service stations, and any other place that has large bare plate-glass windows. They show the photographs and leave a price list. Subjects range from simple bells and holly to complicated manger scenes. Their fee varies according to the size of the picture painted. It covers the cost of paint and a fair hourly rate for their time.

Stage scenery

Another teen-ager paints stage scenery for theater groups.

"I couldn't earn a living at it," Connie says, "but I get paid well for my work." She painted her first set free, but for all the rest she has done she has been paid.

To do this sort of thing, contact the director of the theater group in your city. Offer to do it on a "satisfaction guarantee": if they aren't satisfied, they don't have to pay.

If you furnish paint, be sure to figure the cost of the paint into your fee. You do need some experience in this sort of thing first. Connie had worked with stage scenery for class plays.

Pencil portraits

Sixteen-year-old Claudia earns enough money each summer to buy all of her own clothes by making quick pencil portrait sketches of tourists. She sets up her easel and a hand-lettered sign on the sidewalk of her small resort town. She says it takes her about fifteen minutes to make a sketch for which she gets paid $1. She often has clients waiting in line. Who can resist a portrait for a dollar?

During the school year, she sells sketches of her classmates. She carries a pad and pencil everywhere she goes and sketches for fun. Sometimes her friends buy, sometimes not. "But at least I keep in practice," she says.

Claudia likes to sketch children. "Parents will buy anything that looks remotely like their kids," she says. "Quick sketches are great for little kids because they can't sit still very long."

Other teen-agers make colored chalk, pastel, or charcoal portrait sketches. Claudia likes doing the "quickie sketches" better than finished portraits. "People buy on impulse," she says "and I can make more money doing those. The materials are less expensive and easier to carry."

Cartooning

Twelve-year-old Maynard draws cartoons that he sells to the local newspaper. Maynard got his start cartooning when his sixth-grade teacher suggested he send some of the cartoons, which she thought were hilarious, to the local newspaper instead of decorating his homework with them. He did and the editor liked them, too. He pays a set fee for each one he buys.

"It isn't much, but it keeps me in pocket money," says Maynard. It only takes him fifteen to twenty minutes to draw one. Many of his ideas come from his classmates, but his favorites are inspired by his dog.

If you like to draw cartoons, show them to an adult. If they think the cartoons are funny, select several of your best ones and show them to your local newspaper editor. Use India ink on heavy white bond paper. If the editor likes them, he might buy a few. If he doesn't, he may tell you why he doesn't like them and show you what you can do about it. Or he may tell you about somewhere else you might sell them.

CUSTOM T-SHIRTS—Two fifteen-year-old boys use their artistic talents to paint custom-made designs and slogans on T-shirts. Their customers furnish the T-shirts and frequently the designs. Arne and Chris began by painting the T-shirts they

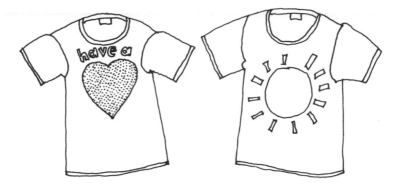

wore to school. The shirts were an instant success. Dozens of classmates wanted similar ones, so the boys were in business.

They now have a portfolio of designs to choose from and also draw designs suggested by the customers. Their specialty, however, is custom-made designs that express the personality of each customer.

Since the boys have no competition in their city, they charge whatever they can get. They haven't needed to advertise because their customers spread the word, and they are as busy as they want to be.

Plenty of people like having clothing that is uniquely theirs, unlike anyone else's. That's why, if you are handy with a brush and pencil, you too can make money custom-painting T-shirts.

These boys use Liquitex acrylic paint and a brush to paint the designs or slogans onto the shirts. This paint can be purchased at any arts and crafts store. Clear instructions for its use are printed on each tube.

You can also use ball-point tube paints which can be purchased at art supply stores. This paint isn't messy and dries in about 2 minutes, but should not be washed for 24 hours.

You could also silk-screen designs. Any good library has books

202

describing this process. Silk screen ink can also be purchased at most arts and crafts stores.

Tips to remember

1. In setting a price for your work, don't forget to figure in the price of the paint plus a reasonable sum for your time.

2. The T-shirts should be washed before painting. Chris and Arne's customers laundered their own shirts before leaving them to be painted. If you do the laundering, add that to the fee.

3. Do not try to do this for pay before you have had some experience. Use your experience to estimate how long it will take you to do a job and determine how much paint will be required. A simple slogan should not cost as much as a complicated design. Give an estimate before you begin.

4. Use examples of your handiwork to advertise. A simple card posted on your school bulletin board can give your telephone number and rates. Word of mouth is the best advertising you can get.

5. To paint the shirts, these boys thumbtack the T-shirts to a 12-inch square of heavy cardboard which they slip up inside the T-shirt. A 12-inch square of wood covered with blotter paper could be used. Be careful not to break a thread when pushing the thumbtack through the shirt.

WRITING—Many young people have earned money through their writing ability. An Oklahoma high school girl covers her school's out-of-town sports events for the local newspaper. She gets paid by the inch for all the copy that is printed. Sometimes she even gets a by-line.

If your community has a small newspaper and you are interested in doing this sort of thing, contact the managing editor and talk to him. Offer to cover three or four events to give him a chance to see what you can do. Then talk pay.

This probably wouldn't work with a big city newspaper which regularly covers all events, but smaller newspapers don't have enough reporters to cover all the sports events, especially if there is more than one school in the area. This won't make you rich, but it is an excellent way to earn pocket money and get valuable experience at the same time. One newspaper hired their high school sports reporter as a regular employee each summer while he attended journalism school.

A junior high school boy used his writing talent to help pay for a ten-speed bike. He sold two poems to his church-school paper for $3 each. Encouraged by this success, he consulted *The Writer's Market* in his public library and submitted poems to all youth magazines that regularly buy poetry from teens.

"I sell maybe one out of fifty," he says. "I'll never become a millionaire, but at least I get more than I had before." For one poem he received a second-place cash prize in a poetry contest.

Other young people have found ways to cash in on their writing talent. A few, like S. E. Hinton, have made thousands of dollars. Susie Hinton sold a best-selling young adult novel to a major book publisher when she was seventeen.

One boy and his roommate earn all their spending money at college by writing stories which they sell to confession magazines. The boys, who are in engineering school, are paid $150 to $300 for each story they sell. It takes about two weeks of their spare time for them to write a good story.

"We buy and read several issues of each magazine in order to see what kind of stories the editors like," they said. "Most of the magazines like stories from a woman's point of view, so we write that kind."

Their story ideas are about problems they or their friends have faced or problems they have read about in the newspaper.

Another boy is a science fiction fan and writes for science fiction magazines. "They don't buy everything I write, but I'm getting better and selling more now," he says.

Sixteen-year-old Trudy rewrites and sells most of her term papers to magazines and newspapers. Her writer mother helps Trudy choose topics for her papers that she thinks might sell. Most of Trudy's articles go to youth magazines.

"Why shouldn't I cash in on my research?" she asks. "I've done all the work myself."

Mary sold her first story to *Seventeen*, a magazine that annually sponsors a contest for teen-aged writers. Kathryn sold a poem to a church magazine for $15 and a personal experience article to *American Girl* for $25.

If you are a talented writer, cash in on it. Your local library probably has a copy of *The Writer's Market*. If it doesn't, suggest to the head librarian that it would be a good reference book to order.

ORIGINAL GREETING CARDS—Sixteen-year-old Renée's handmade original greeting cards were so popular among her friends that they began asking her to make special cards for them. "I did that for a while. The kids paid me whatever they wanted to. Then someone suggested that I send some of my ideas to a greeting card company," she says. The first company bought two of them. Now she submits ideas regularly.

Renée prefers the humorous "studio" type, the kind with a gag line, but has also sold some verse. She also continues to take orders for her hand-drawn and hand-lettered originals.

Tips
1. Study cards at the local card shops to see what is being

sold. Find out what kind your friends prefer. "My friends generate most of my ideas," Renée says.

2. Look for a handbook on greeting-card writing at your library. Writers' magazines are also good sources of information.

3. Send 10 to 12 ideas at a time. As with any writing, always include a self-addressed and stamped envelope for returning unsold material.

4. Keep a copy of each idea and a record of the company to which it was sent.

5. Do not expect to sell every idea. Renée says she sells about one out of ten, and that is a fair average.

6. You can find a list of more than thirty greeting card companies in *The Writer's Market*. Study the company's needs. Not all companies buy the same types.

EMBROIDERING JEANS AND JACKETS—Almost every kid who knows Janice has a jean jacket she has embroidered. It all started when Janice embroidered a 6-inch thunderbird on the back of her brother's jacket for his birthday. His friends loved it and asked her to embroider their personal symbols on the back of their jackets. That's when 14-year-old Janice went into business.

Customers with artistic ability draw their own designs for Janice to copy. For others, she both draws and embroiders the designs they want. She and her customers work out the designs in crayon on graph paper; then Janice transfers the designs to the jackets. She uses a satin stitch to fill in all areas of the designs. Janice asks her customers to supply their own thread, so she charges only for her work. She knows by the size of the design about how long it will take her to do the work and gives an estimate before she starts.

"A very elaborate design can get pretty expensive," she says. "I try to get my customers to keep it simple. It's less expensive, and I think it looks better."

Tips for embroidering

1. Lots of boys and girls have made money embroidering. Most kids can't or don't like to embroider, but do like to have their clothes personalized. That's why it is a good way for you to earn money.

Although Janice specializes in jackets, others embroider anything from shirts and jeans to pillowcases. If you like to embroider, put an ad in your school paper or a sign on the bulletin board.

This is how one boy worded his ad:

NEEDLE FOR HIRE
Custom embroidery
Your design or mine
Call Morris
662-2875

2. You might like to specialize, too. One girl says she will embroider anything but jean jackets. "They are too hard to work on," she says. Cambric shirts are her favorite. "They are so much easier to embroider, and I can use a greater variety of stitches and designs."

3. Leslie specializes in wall hangings. These are something like old-fashioned samplers, except that she uses a variety of stitches instead of just the cross-stitch. The hangings include a favorite verse or slogan decorated with original designs.

Leslie started making these hangings as gifts for special friends. Then her friends began asking her to make hangings that they could give as gifts. The samplers are treasured because they always depict some important point in the life of the person who will receive it. For example, the hanging Leslie embroidered for a girl who went steady with a rodeo calf-roper contained the verse of the recipient's favorite cowboy song. The verse was surrounded by bucking broncos, steers, calves, and cactus.

Leslie's customers supply the words and sometimes help work out the designs, then she transfers it all onto unbleached muslin and embroiders it. Sometimes instead of being framed, the pieces are made into pillows. Leslie says you could use transfer patterns for illustrations if you wanted.

4. Some people do beautiful machine-embroidery work. If you have access to a sewing machine with embroidering attachments and are skilled in using them, you can earn money with it. Many people who never learned to embroider, or who just don't want to bother, like to have initials embroidered on towels, pillowcases, sheets, and handkerchiefs. Hand-embroidered monogrammed sheets and pillowcases make an elegant wedding gift. Mothers often like to have designs stitched on small children's clothing. If you place an ad in a community bulletin and keep your fees reasonable, you will get lots of calls.

5. Having customers supply their own thread will make it easier for you to give an estimate of the cost before you start. It also saves you the wear and tear of trying to find the exact color wanted.

6. Always give an estimate before starting. It is bad business for a customer to find out after you have done the work that it is much more expensive than expected.

SEWING—Fourteen-year-old Barbara is a creative seamstress. She has been sewing since she was nine. She started by selling doll clothes because she enjoyed designing and sewing them. "It was the only way I could get away with dressing dolls at my age," she laughs. But what started with doll clothes has grown to include every kind of stuffed animal you could imagine, from gingham goats to calico cats. She sells all her doll clothes and some of her stuffed animals to individuals through ads in the community shoppers' guide. However, most of her stuffed animals are sold through a store which sells them on consignment. That is, they keep a percentage of the sale price.

Barbara's first doll clothes and stuffed animals were made from scrap materials left over from her own wardrobe. Now she buys bundles of scraps at garage sales and remnants at discount stores.

At first Barbara used patterns that she bought or borrowed,

but now she makes many of her own designs. Her favorites are stuffed animals made from plush or fake fur, and cuddly animal pillows.

Barbara's busiest seasons are Christmas and Easter. For Easter, she makes up dozens of gaily colored rabbits and ducks.

Tips for doing it yourself

1. If you like to sew and have access to a sewing machine, ask friends and neighbors who sew to save their fabric scraps for you.

2. To save expenses when starting, use old nylon stockings and the stocking part of panty hose for stuffing. "I begged old hose from everyone," says Barbara. Now she uses part of her profits to buy shredded foam for stuffing.

3. Any fabric scrap can be used, but small children like bright colors.

4. Stuffed animals and pillows are popular with the college crowd, too. Think college themes for some of your creations.

5. Use only one or two basic patterns when starting. Make up no more than five or six at a time. When you have sold those, make more. Use your profits to expand.

6. When making doll clothes, sew for a doll that is popular. Barbara makes clothes for fashion dolls. One of her best sellers is a fur coat made from fake fur.

7. Barbara displays doll clothes by fastening basic styles on cardboard with masking tape and covering them with plastic wrap. This makes it much easier for little girls to make selections. Since Barbara has little overhead, she can price the clothes and animals low enough that she sells large numbers of them.

8. She advertises in the newspaper. Her ad includes a price list.

TALKING—Fifteen-year-old Nicole talked herself into a $500 scholarship by winning top honors in an international oration contest. This takes a special kind of talent and only one or two can win each year. But this is not the only way to earn money talking. Many teen-agers have used their talking ability to earn a regular income.

Radio disc jockey

Fifteen-year-old Ferris has the gift of gab. He talked the manager of his local radio station into letting him be a disc jockey three mornings a week for the entire summer. He was a big hit with the listeners. The station manager asked him to work on Saturdays during the school year and rehired him full time the next summer.

Another boy does radio reports of Little League baseball games, events not normally covered by the regular radio staff. He does so well that he has been offered the opportunity of covering the junior high sports events during the school year.

TV opportunities

A 13-year-old boy and an 11-year-old girl were paid the same salary as adults for reporting news about other kids on a television show in San Francisco one summer.

Many smaller radio or television stations welcome summer replacements while their regular staff people are on vacation. If you think you have a talent for this sort of work, call your local radio or television station and make an appointment with the manager. Outline your show idea to him and offer to do one or two free. It will be good experience even if he doesn't hire you.

One boy's job-winning idea for a television show was to interview other local teen-agers to find out their views on current events and local issues. He also interviewed teen-agers who had done something newsworthy, such as rescuing someone, winning an award, or receiving a scholarship.

MODELING—You don't have to be a professional model to earn money modeling. Teen-agers in smaller cities earn pocket money modeling for amateur photography clubs and art classes. You needn't be beautiful or handsome for this, but you do have to be able to hold still for long periods of time.

Sometimes dress shops hire local teen-agers to model clothing in style shows given for civic organizations. Some hire models to stand in the windows to display clothing. This is the kind of work Angie does.

"Freeze modeling is the hardest job," says the fifteen-year-old. "You have to hold perfectly still and look like a manikin. We really attract a lot of attention. People do all sorts of things to try to get us to move. It's a challenge. I enjoy doing it, but I don't want to make a career of it. It doesn't pay enough."

If you would like to try modeling, contact your local photography clubs and art associations. Ask to be placed on their model list. Ask clothing-store managers to put you on their list of available models.

EXERCISE CLASS—Edith and Willa teach a pounds-off class for weight-conscious people. These 16-year-olds have 15 members in their class. Members are charged $6 for an 8-week session. The girls lead members in exercises in time to music provided by a record player. They meet for one hour, once a week.

To add incentive, members who lose at least 4 pounds by the end of 4 weeks, or 8 pounds at the end of 8 weeks are refunded $1. Most of their members are housewives, but some are overweight classmates. The class is so successful, the girls have a waiting list for membership. They divide all proceeds equally.

Suggestions for using this idea

1. Instead of a reducing class, you could organize a physical-fitness class. Many people are interested in exercising for reasons other than weight control. Go solo or ask a friend to help.

2. Although Edith and Willa were asked to form their class by a group of weight-conscious women, and therefore did not need to advertise, you could advertise for students. Place post-

ers on school bulletin boards, and announcements in your community's free consumer's bulletin or in your church bulletin. Also pass the word among your friends and your parents' friends.

3. Use exercises you have learned in gym classes at school or similar places.

4. A driveway or patio can be used for workouts on warm days; a heated garage or basement on cold days. If your membership is large, perhaps you could get permission to use the Fellowship Hall in your church.

5. If you have the time to spare, conduct two sessions a week. Benefit customers as well as your pocketbook.

6. Conduct two classes, one for children and one for adults or teens. The more classes you teach, the more money you can earn.

Index

218